Two Accounts of the Battle of Sedan, 1st September 1870

Two Accounts of the Battle of Sedan, 1st September 1870

The Battle of Sedan

By George W. A. Fitz-George

Battlefield of Sedan

C. W. Robinson

LEONAUR

Two Accounts of the Battle of Sedan, 1st September 1870
The Battle of Sedan
by George W. A. Fitz-George
and
Battlefield of Sedan
by C. W. Robinson

First published under the titles

The Plan of the Battle of Sedan Accompanied by a Short Memoir
and
Battlefield of Sedan, and a Fortnight with the German Armies in Lorraine

Leonaur is an imprint of Oakpast Ltd

Copyright in this form © 2011 Oakpast Ltd

ISBN: 978-0-85706-697-8 (hardcover)
ISBN: 978-0-85706-698-5 (softcover)

http://www.leonaur.com

Publisher's Notes

Contents

The Battle of Sedan

By George W. A. Fitz-George

Contents

Preface

In offering the Memoir to the public, I am fully conscious how far my humble efforts fall short of what is due to the subject I have taken in hand; but whatever be the shortcomings in them, I shall feel that I have not quite worked in vain if I succeed in interesting or conveying the least information to my readers.

I must not omit to acknowledge my obligations to the able and spirited war correspondence of the London Press, as well as to the Correspondents I had the good fortune to meet at Sedan, to whose encouragement this modest brochure mainly owes its publication.

G. Fitz-George.

London, 23rd April, 1871.

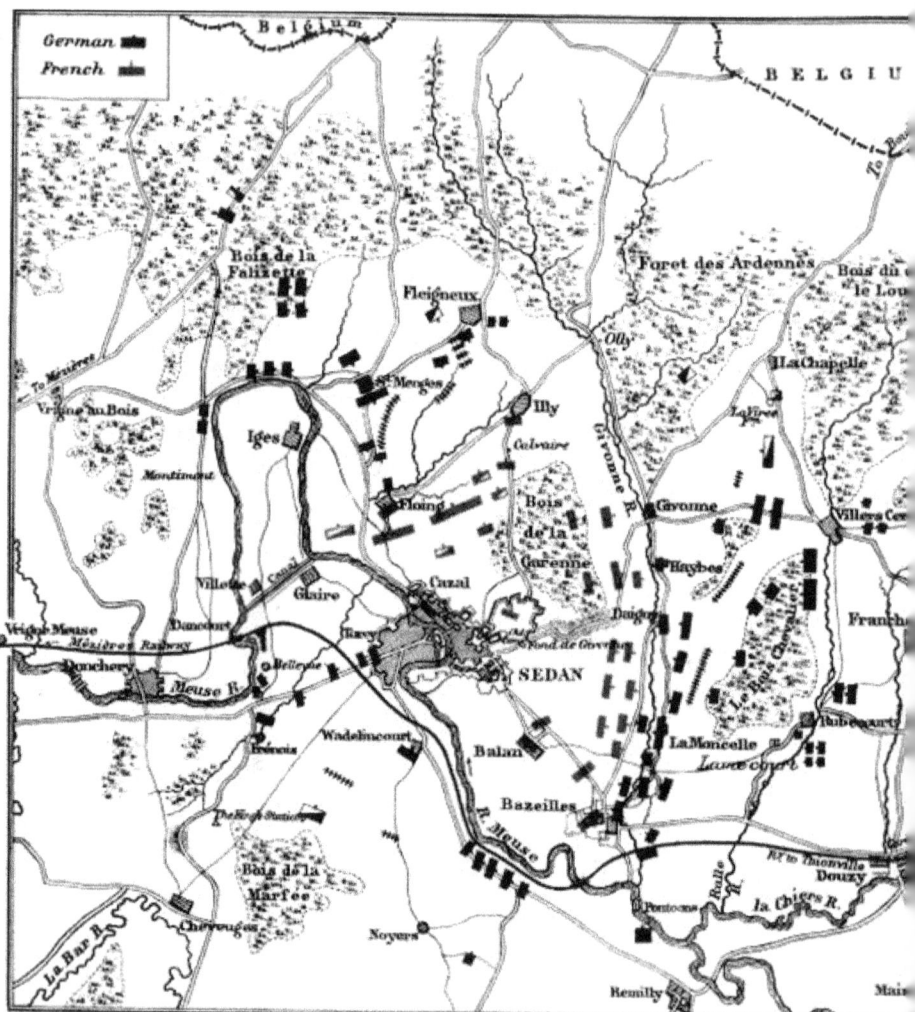

German ■■■
French ■■■

BELGIUM

BELGIU

To Pa

To Mezieres

BELGIUM

Bois de la
Falizette

Fleigneux

Foret des Ardennes

Bois du c
le Lou

Olly

IlaChapelle

LaFire

Vrigne au Bois

Mengles

Illy

Iges

Calvaire

Gironne R.

Villers Cer

Montimont

Floing

Bois
de la
Garenne

Gironne

Haybes

Villette

Glaire

Canal

Daigny

Franch

Vrigne Meuse

Cazal

Donchery

Daucourt

Bazey

Bellevue

Fond de Govev

Meuse R.

Mezieres Railway

SEDAN

La Moncelle

Aubecourt

Lance court

Francois

Wadelincourt

Balan

Petit Station

Bazeilles

Rl to Thisnville

Douzy

Bois de la
Marfee

R. Meuse

Route

Pontoon

la Chiers R.

Le Bar R.

Chevenges

Noyers

Reuilly

Mair

Memoir of the Battle of Sedan

The culminating disaster that befell the Imperial army of France, in the recent campaign, was fated to take place in the vicinity of the fortified town of Sedan, a place probably unknown, by name even, to most Englishmen until the telegrams in the newspapers announced the total overthrow of MacMahon's army, and the surrender of the Emperor Napoleon III. and of the survivors of the terrible conflict fought there on the 1st September, 1870.

Although the fall of Metz, and the surrender of Bazaine with the Imperial Guard and the bulk of the remainder of the original Imperial army, to the troops of Prince Frederick Charles, were subsequent to the battle of Sedan, still, inasmuch as the Imperial dynasty was formally deposed in Paris on the 4th September, 1870, I consider the surrender of the 1st the final disaster that befell the armies of the third Napoleon.

In the *Edinburgh Gazetteer* we find:

Sedan, a considerable town in the north-east of France, department of the Ardennes. It is situated on the right bank of the Meuse, and is strongly fortified, being surrounded with walls, bastions, ditches, and other works, constructed partly by Vauban. The old castle, in which Turenne was born, is now converted into an arsenal, and is one of the best in France. The town is divided into Upper and Lower; and, though not badly built, is, from the uneven and rocky nature of the ground which it occupies, very irregular. Of the population, in number nearly 11,000, a part are Protestants. Sedan has been long noted for its manufactures of superfine woollens, and for a very different branch of industry, the making of firearms and copper articles; it has likewise a cannon foundry. Sedan was formerly the seat of a Protestant University. 37 miles S.E. of Charlemont, and 170

13

N.E. of Paris. Long. 4° 57' 50" E., lat. 49° 42' 29" N.

The above was written in 1827.

Johnston's *Gazetteer* in 1859 gives a population of 16,759, and at the present day, (at time of first publication), including the suburbs, it has about 20,000 inhabitants.

Sedan is one of three fortresses—namely, Sedan, Mézières, and Montmédy—originally constructed to meet and check any invasion of France from Belgian territory, and is the principal town in the fourth *arrondissement* of the department of the Ardennes, being situated on the east bank of the Meuse, about 160 miles north-east of Paris.

The fortress is constructed on a combination of Vauban's different systems, and a few years back could have stood a long siege; but the improvements in modern artillery have rendered it untenable, owing to the high ground unfortified that environs it, and at present it is only a *cul-de-sac* for any shot or shell that may be projected against it from the surrounding heights.

It is built on an uneven site, surrounded by meadows, *châteaux*, and cultivated fields, and has an admirable defensive system of inundations and wet ditches, the water for which is obtained from the Meuse, which winds picturesquely through the southern part of the town.

The hospital stands out prominently on the north side, while the citadel is on an eminence to the south-east. There are also an arsenal, and three large barracks, besides stores and officers' quarters.

The fortress is overlooked by masses of dark forest; and, while here and there may be seen large plateaux, the surrounding hills, more especially on the north side, are broken into deep and precipitous gorges; and the rivers Meuse and Chiers, and numerous smaller streams, winding fantastically here and there, form an intricate network of obstacles difficult for an army to overcome, when faced by a determined and skilful adversary.

Commercially the town is noted for its woollen, cloth, linen, and numerous other manufactures; while historically it is associated with the names of Henry IV., Louis XIY., and of Marshal Turenne—who was born there, and whose statue is one of the local objects of interest.

The positions of the different corps constituting the French army, and their relative strength in men and guns at the opening of the campaign, were as follows:—

1st Corps, under Marshal MacMahon, consisting of 90 guns, 3,500 cavalry, and 35,000 infantry, at Strasbourg.

2nd Corps, under General Froissard, 72 guns, 2,600 cavalry, and 26,250 infantry, at St. Avoid.

4th Corps, under General L'Admirault, of similar strength, at Thionville;

And the 5th Corps, under General De Failly, also of similar strength, at Bitche.

The advanced line, therefore, forming a total of 306 guns, 11,300 cavalry, and 113,750 infantry.

IN SUPPORT.

The 3rd Corps, comprising 90 guns, 3,500 cavalry, and 35,000 infantry, under Marshal Bazaine, at Metz.

The Imperial Guard, consisting of 60 guns, 3,600 cavalry, and 16,650 infantry, under General Bourbaki, at Nancy.

IN RESERVE.

At Châlons:—The cavalry reserve, numbering 36 guns and 6,250 sabres; and the 6th Corps, comprising 90 guns, 3,500 cavalry, and 35,000 infantry, under Marshal Canrobert.

At Belfort:—The 7th Corps, numbering 72 guns, 2,600 cavalry, and 26,500 infantry, under General Felix Douay.

The whole forming a grand total of

Guns.	Cavalry.	Infantry.
654	30,750	226,900

The French position strategically viewed was thus as follows:—

Strasbourg, Bitche, St. Avoid, Metz, and Thionville were on one line of railway.

Strasbourg had also railway communication with Nancy and Metz by Saverne, Sarrebourg, and Lunéville; and with Belfort to its rear.

Nancy communicated with Paris by Vitry and Châlons; and Thionville with Paris by Montmédy, Mézières, and Rheims.

Thus the whole front towards Germany had ample railway connection, and from different points along the French line railways were available to concentrate troops in rear or on the flanks.

Strasbourg was the base of operations for the French right, and

Metz for the centre and left.

Besides Strasbourg and Metz other frontier fortresses strengthened the advanced line—Bitche and Phalsbourg in the Vosges, and Thionville on the Moselle.

The French army occupied, therefore, a very long line, and its advanced corps, extending from Thionville on the left to Strasbourg on the right, were scattered over too wide a front, insufficiently connected, and too far from their supports at Metz; and, as the result proved, were liable to be beaten in detail and cut off from each other. Had the French organized their troops rapidly at the above places, and then, concentrating at some point, crossed the Rhine and separated Southern from Northern Germany, a different *finale* might have been the result of initiating the war in the enemy's country; but scattered along so wide a front, and ill-informed by its scouts, the French army was strategically in a very dangerous position. It is believed that the Emperor's original plan of the campaign was as follows:—

To concentrate at Metz and Strasbourg, and form his reserves at Châlons—thus leaving the enemy in doubt as to his point of crossing the frontier.

The armies from Metz and Strasbourg were then to be combined, and crossing the Rhine at Maxau, leaving Rastadt on their right, to cut the communication between Northern and Southern Germany. The reserves were to follow and protect the rear of the French and also the eastern frontier.

The French fleet were to cruise in the Baltic, thus detaining a large German force to watch the coast.

The delay in the organization of the different French corps, and the bad system of men joining their regimental *depôts* instead of proceeding at once to their stations—added to the pernicious system of extreme centralization that prevailed, and the fact that the materiel was stored in different cities in enormous magazines instead of being convenient to the districts requiring it, in consequence of which many things lumbered up the railways, never reaching their destination, and numerous regiments entered on the campaign deficient of *tentes d'abri*, havresacks, camp-kettles, &c.—all conduced to upset the Emperor's plan, the only chance of success for which was in surpassing the enemy in rapidity of movement.

The German armies consisted of the 1st, or Army of the Saar, under General von Steinmetz, comprising the 7th Corps of Westphalians, under General von Zastrow; the 8th Rhinelanders, under General von Göben; part of the 10th Corps; and the Brandenburg division of cavalry; total strength, 70,000 men, and 186 guns.

The 1st Army occupied the line of the Saar, from Saarburg on the right, to Saarbrücken; while its supports were at Ottweiler, Homburg, and Landstuhl, in the vicinity of the railway to Saarbrücken.

The 2nd, or Army of the Rhine, under Prince Frederick Charles of Prussia, comprising the 1st East Prussian Corps, under General Manteuffel; the 2nd Pomeranian, under General Fransetzky; the 3rd Brandenburger, under General von Alvensleben II.; the 4th Prussians, Saxons, and Thuringians, under General von Alvensleben I.; the 9th Schleswig Holstein, under General von Manstein; the 10th Hanoverians, under General von Voigts Rhetz; the 12th Saxons, under the Crown Prince of Saxony; the Hesse Darmstadt division; the Garrison of Mayence (Mainz); and the 1st, 2nd, 4th, 10th, and 12th cavalry divisions; making a total of 250,000 men, with 660 guns.

The above having crossed the Rhine at Mayence and Mannheim, prolonged the line to the left by Zweibrücken, and held Kaiserslautern and Neustadt in force.

And the 3rd, or Army of the South, under the Crown Prince of Prussia, consisting of the Corps of the Guard, under Prince Augustus of Würtemburg; the 5th Poseners, under General von Kirchbach; the 6th Silesians, under General von Tümpling; the 11th Hesse and Nassau, under General von Böse; the Würtemburg contingent, under Lieutenant-General von Obernitz; the Baden contingent, under General von Beyer; the Bavarian contingent, under General von der Tann; and the 6th cavalry division: making a total of 250,000 men, with 660 guns.

This army occupied the junction of the railways which come from Neustadt and Carlsruhe, and occupied Landau, Neustadt, and Spire with its reserves.

These three German armies formed a grand total of about 570,000 men, with 1,506 guns, and strategically were admirably disposed to defend their country from the invader. Although the system of railways on their side was hardly as complete as on the French side, yet the superior organization existing on the German lines compensated for any advantage on that score. General Steinmetz had a railway along his front, commencing at Trèves (Trier), and connecting with Prince Frederick Charles's position by Homburg; while the Crown Prince of Prussia had railway communication with the 2nd Army by Neustadt and Landau; and the whole line extended from Saarburg on the right to a junction called Wenden on the left; and as the railways between those points are concave to the French frontier, the lines were available with safety for rapid concentration at any point. There were several lines of retreat by rail available for each army, and the position was strengthened by the fortresses of Mayence, Landau, and Germersheim.

I append lists, containing fuller details of the forces of the French and German armies, taken from an account by a staff officer published shortly after the commencement of the campaign. While I do not vouch for their correctness, I believe the totals shown in the tabular estimates to be reconcilable with the figures I have already given; especially when we take into consideration the difficulties all writers laboured under at the beginning of the campaign, from the hostility of the commanders to all who did not belong to either army; especially to those who, by their statistics and military criticisms, might have afforded indirectly information to the enemy.

FRENCH ARMY.

The 1st Corps d'Armée. MARSHAL MACMAHON.

Chef d'Etat Major, Colson, Gen. de Brigade.
Chef d'Artillerie, Forgeot, Gen. de Brigade.

	Battalions, or Squadrons.	Guns.	Combatants.	
			Infantry.	Cavalry.
1st Division. Ducrot, Gen. de Div.				
Two brigades —				
1 battalion of Chasseurs, 4 regiments of the line	13	..	8,750	..
Artillery, 2 batteries	..	12	..	..
Total	13	12	8,750	..
2nd Division. Abel Douay, Gen. de Div.				
Two brigades—				
1 battalion of Chasseurs, 2 regiments of the line	7	..	4,750	..
1 ditto of Zouaves, 1 ditto of Turcos.. ..	6	..	4,500	..
Artillery, 2 batteries	..	12	..	..
Total	13	12	9,250	..
3rd Division. Raoult, Gen. de Div.				
Two brigades—				
1 battalion of Chasseurs, 2 regiments of the line	7	..	4,750	..
1 ditto of Zouaves, 1 ditto of Turcos ..	6	..	4,500	..
Artillery, 2 batteries	..	12	..	..
Total	13	12	9,250	..

	Battalions, or Squadrons.	Guns.	Combatants.	
			Infantry.	Cavalry.
4th Division. Lartigues, Gen. de Div.				
Two brigades—				
1 battalion of Chasseurs, 2 regiments of the line	7	..	4,750	..
1 ditto of Zouaves, 1 ditto of Turcos ..	6	..	4,500	..
Artillery, 2 batteries	..	12	..	..
Total	13	12	9,250	..
Cavalry Div. Duhesme, Gen. de Div.				
Three brigades—				
1st Brigade, 1 regiment of Hussars, 1 Chasseurs à cheval	28	..	..	3,640
2nd „ 1 regt. of Lancers, 1 Dragoons				
3rd „ 2 „ Cuirassiers				
Artillery, 2 batteries	..	12	..	..
Total	28	12	..	3,640
Artillery reserve of this corps, 5 batteries	..	30	..	..
Grand total of 1st *Corps d'Armée* ..	‡‡	90	36,500	3,640

The 2nd Corps d'Armée. LIEUT.-GENERAL DE FROSSARD.

Chef d'Etat Major, Saget, Gen. de Brigade.
Chef d'Artillerie, Gagneur, Gen. de Brigade.

	Battalions, or Squadrons.	Guns.	Combatants.	
			Infantry.	Cavalry.
1st Division. Vergé, Gen. de Div.				
Two brigades—				
1 battalion of Chasseurs, 4 regiments of the line	13	..	8,750	..
Artillery, 2 batteries	..	12	..	..
Total	13	12	8,750	..
2nd Division. Bataille, Gen. de Div., same formation and strength..	13	12	8,750	..
3rd Div. Laveau-Coupet, Gen. de Div., ditto	13	12	8,750	..
Cavalry Division. Letellier, Gen. de Div., 1 brigade Chasseurs, 1 ditto Dragoons, 4 regiments, 2 batteries	16	12	..	2,080
Artillery reserve of this corps, 4 batteries	..	24	..	..
Grand total of 2nd *Corps d'Armée* ..	‡‡	72	26,250	2,080

The 3rd Corps d'Armée. MARSHAL BAZAINE.

Chef d'Etat Major, Maneque, Gen. de Brigade de Artillerie.
De Rochebouet, Gen. de Brigade.

		Battalions, or Squadrons.	Guns.	Combatants.	
				Infantry.	Cavalry.
1st Division.	Montandon, Gen. de Div...	13	12	8,750	..
2nd „	De Castagny „ „ ..	13	12	8,750	..
3rd „	Metman „ „ ..	13	12	8,750	..
4th „	Decaen „ „ ..	13	12	8,750	..
Cavalry—					
1st Brigade.	3 regiments of Chasseurs ..				
2nd „	2 „ of Dragoons ..	28	12	..	3,640
3rd „	2 „ of „ ..				
Artillery reserve of corps like 1st Corps..		..	30	..	..
Grand total 3rd *Corps d'Armée*		⁴⁴⁄₁₃	90	35,000	3,640

The 4th Corps d'Armée. LIEUT.-GENERAL DE L'ADMIRAULT.

Chef d'Etat Major, Besson, Gen. de Brigade.
Chef d'Artillerie, Lafaille, Gen. de Brigade.
1st Division, De Cissey; 2nd, Rose; 3rd, De Lorencez;
Cavalry—Legrand, Generaux de Division.

	Battalions, or Squadrons.	Guns.	Combatants.	
			Infantry.	Cavalry.
Same strength and composition as the 2nd Corps	⁴⁴⁄₁₃	72	26,250	2,080

The 5th Corps d'Armée. LIEUT.-GENERAL DE FAILLY.

Chef d'Etat Major, Besson, Gen. de Brigade.
Chef d'Artillerie, Liodot, Gen. de Brigade.
1st Division, Goze; 2nd, De l'Abadie; 3rd, Guyot;
Cavalry—Brahans, Generaux de Division.

	Battalions, or Squadrons.	Guns.	Combatants.	
			Infantry.	Cavalry.
Same strength and composition as the 4th Corps	⁴⁴⁄₁₃	72	26,250	2,080

The Imperial Guard. LIEUT.-GENERAL BOURBAKI.

Chef d'Etat Major, d'Auvergne, Gen. de Division.
Chef d'Artillerie, Pe d'Arros, Gen. de Brigade.

	Battalions, or Squadrons.	Guns.	Combatants.	
			Infantry.	Cavalry.
1st Division. De Ligny, Gen. de Div.				
Two brigades—				
1 battalion of Chasseurs	1	..	850	..
4 regiments of Voltigeurs	12	..	7,200	..
Artillery, 2 batteries	..	..	..	..
Total	13	12	8,050	..
2nd Division. Picard, Gen. de Div.				
Two brigades—				
Regiments of Zouaves	2	..	3,000	..
3 regiments of Grenadiers	9	..	5,400	..
Artillery, 2 batteries	..	12	..	..
Total	11	12	8,400	..
Cavalry Division. Devaux, Gen. de Div.				
1st brigade, 1 reg. Chasseurs, 1 ditto Guides	8	..	..	1,200
2nd „ 1 „ Dragoons, 1 „ Lancers	8	..	..	1,200
3rd „ 1 „ Carabineers, 1 Cuirassiers	8	..	..	1,200
Artillery, 2 batteries	..	12	..	..
Total	24	12	..	3,600
Artillery reserve of the Imperial Guard, 4 batteries .. .. }	..	24	..	..
Grand total, Imperial Guard	4⅔	60	16,450	3,600

The 6th Corps. MARSHAL CANROBERT.

	Battalions, or Squadrons.	Guns.	Combatants.	
			Infantry.	Cavalry.
1st Division of cavalry } Probably 1 light {	16	12	..	3,600
2nd „ „ } division and 2 {	16	12	..	3,600
3rd „ „ } heavy ditto .. {	16	12	..	3,600
1 division of infantry	13	12	8,750	..
Artillery reserve, probably 5 to 6 batteries, say 6 .. .. }	..	30	..	..
Grand total 6th Corps d'Armée	4⅔	78	8,750	10,800

"The 7th Corps is said to be in course of formation, under General Felix Douay, with troops that still remain in Algeria, from whence about 18,000 men of the 1st Corps have been already withdrawn. The division hitherto in garrison at Borne will also be available, it seems. This corps, when formed, will probably have the same composition and strength as the 2nd and 4th Corps.

"The sum total of the Army of the Rhine will therefore be, according to our mode of reckoning, merely the combatants of the infantry and cavalry, and the guns of the artillery, as follows:—

	Batta-lions.	Squad-rons.	Guns.	Combatants.	
				Infantry.	Cavalry.
1st *Corps d'Armée* in the 1st line	52	28	90	36,500	3,640
2nd ,, ,, ,, ...	39	16	72	26,250	2,080
3rd ,, ,, ,, ...	52	28	90	35,000	3,640
4th ,, ,, ,, ...	39	16	72	26,250	2,080
5th ,, ,, ,, ...	39	16	72	26,250	2,080
Total 1st line	221	104	396	150,250	13,520
Imperial Guard—as reserve	24	24	60	16,650	3,600
6th *Corps d'Armée*	13	48	78	8,750	10,800
Total reserve	37	72	138	25,400	14,400
Grand total	258	176	534	175,650	27,920

203,570

Add to this for the artillery	17,000	
,, ,, engineers	4,000	
,, ,, train	5,000	
,, ,, non-combatants ..	4,000	

30,000

And we have in the field 233,570

The smaller number of infantry shown here can be accounted for by the supposition that there were more regiments of *Zouaves* in the field forces than the compiler of the above allowed for; and, to explain my meaning, I must state that a regiment of *Zouaves* has three battalions, whereas a regiment of *Chasseurs* has but one.

He has also understated the numbers of the cavalry and artillery, under the supposition that the squadrons and batteries were more under their war establishments than they really were.

	Batta-lions.	Squad-rons.	Guns.	Combatants. Infantry.	Combatants. Cavalry.
The *Corps d'Armée* of the Guard.— Prince Augustus of Würtemburg.					
1st Division, Infantry. 1st brigade of infantry, 2 regiments	6	..	..	6,000	..
2nd brigade of infantry, 3 regiments	9	..	..	9,000	..
1 regiment of light cavalry	..	4	..	..	550
1 division of foot artillery, 4 batteries	..	..	24	..	..
Total 1st Division ..	15	4	24	15,000	550
2nd Division, Infantry. 3rd brigade of infantry, 2 regiments	6	..	..	6,000	..
4th brigade of infantry, 2 regiments	6	..	..	6,000	..
1 regiment of light cavalry	..	4	..	..	550
1 division of foot artillery, 4 batteries	..	..	24	..	..
Total 2nd Division ..	12	4	24	12,000	550
Cavalry Division. 1 brigade heavy cavalry, 2 regiments	..	8	..	..	1,100
1 brigade light cavalry, 2 regiments	..	8	..	..	1,100
1 brigade light cavalry, 2 regiments	..	8	..	..	1,100
Horse artillery, 2 batteries	..	..	8	..	..
Total Cavalry Division	..	24	8	..	3,300
Artillery Reserve. 3rd foot division, 4 battalions	..	..	24	..	..
3rd horse artillery, 4 battalions	..	..	16	..	..
1 battalion Jäger of the guard ..	1	..	..	1,000	..
1 battalion sharpshooters of the guard	1	..	..	1,000	..
Total Guards	29	32	96	29,000	4,400

	Batta-lions.	Squad-rons.	Guns.	Combatants.	
				Infantry.	Cavalry.
The 1st Corps, Lieut.-General von Manteuffel.					
Infantry {1st Division	12	..	24	12,000	..
{2nd Division	12	..	24	12,000	..
Jäger, 1 battalion	1	..	..	1,000	..
Cavalry, 6 regiments, with horse artillery 2 battalions .. ..}	..	24	8	..	3,300
Artillery reserve	..	..	40	..	..
Grand total 1st Corps	25	24	96	25,000	3,300
The 2nd Corps, Lieut.-General von Fransetzky .. ..}	25	24	96	25,000	3,300
The 5th Corps, Lieut.-General von Kirchbach .. ..}	25	24	96	25,000	3,300
The 6th Corps, Lieut.-General von Tümpling .. ..}	25	24	96	25,000	3,300
The 7th Corps, Lieut.-General von Zastrow .. ..}	25	24	96	25,000	3,300
The 8th Corps, Lieut.-General von Göben .. ..}	25	24	96	25,000	3,300
The 10th Corps, Lieut.-General von Voigts Rhetz .. ..}	25	24	96	25,000	3,300
The 3rd Corps,* Lieut.-General von Alvensleben II. .. ..}	28	24	96	28,000	3,300
The 4th Corps,† Lieut.-General von Alvensleben I. .. ..}	31	24	96	31,000	3,300
The 9th Corps,‡ Lieut.-General von Manstein .. ..}	29	24	96	29,000	3,300
The 11th Corps, Lieut.-General von Böse, has 3 infantry divisions, and 3 Jäger battalions, with but 2 regiments of cavalry .. ..}	35	8	96	35,000	1,100
The 12th Corps, the Crown Prince of Saxony, with 1 extra infantry regiment and 2 Jäger battalions}	29	24	96	29,000	3,300
Total of the North German Confederation, including Guards ..}	356	304	1,248	356,000	41,800

* 1 brigade has 3 regiments.   † 2 brigades have 3 regiments each.
‡ This corps has 2 Jäger regiments and 1 brigade with 3 regiments.

"Supposing that two of these *Corps d'Armée* be retained in the north of Germany for the defence of the coasts, that is to say, the 9th and 10th in Schleswig and Hanover, the sum total of these would be 54,000 infantry, 6,600 cavalry combatants, and 192 guns, which being deducted from the total of the North German Confederation Army, would leave the latter 302,000 infantry, 35,200 cavalry combatants, with 1,056 guns, to oppose to the French Army on the Rhine. To this force, however, must be added the troops of Southern Germany, that is to say, Bavaria, Würtemburg, and Baden.

"Bavaria can bring into the field two corps with four infantry divisions of two brigades each, the brigade consisting of two infantry regiments and one *Jäger* battalion (with a battery of six guns); and in addition to this, ten regiments of cavalry, of four field squadrons each, with twenty-eight foot and four horse batteries.

"The Bavarian Field Army amounts altogether to—

	Batta-lions.	Squad-rons.	Guns.	Combatants.	
				Infantry.	Cavalry.
Infantry of the line, 16 regiments	48	..	..	45,000	..
Jäger	8	..	..	5,000	..
Cavalry	..	40	..	..	5,000
Artillery batteries, 32	..	..	192	..	..
Total in 2 *Corps d'Armée* ..	56	40	192	50,000	5,000

"The Würtemburg Division consists of one division, three brigades of infantry, one division of cavalry, and nine batteries of artillery, *viz.*:—

	Batta-lions.	Squad-rons.	Guns.	Combatants.	
				Infantry.	Cavalry.
Infantry of the line, 8 regiments	16	..	..	16,000	..
Jäger	3	..	..	3,000	..
Cavalry, 4 regiments	..	16	..	..	2,500
Artillery, 9 batteries	..	..	54	..	..
Total Würtemburg Division ..	19	16	54	19,000	2,500

"The Division of the Grand Duchy of Baden:—

	Batta-lions.	Squad-rons.	Guns.	Combatants.	
				Infantry.	Cavalry.
Infantry, 6 regiments	18	..	..	18,000	..
Cavalry, 3 regiments	..	12	..	..	1,800
Artillery, 7 batteries	..	..	42	..	..
Total Baden Division	18	12	42	18,000	1,800

"The entire Field Force of the north and south of Germany may therefore be thus calculated:—

	Batta-lions.	Squad-rons.	Guns.	Combatants.	
				Infantry.	Cavalry.
9th and 10th *Corps d'Armée* for defence of Northern Coasts ..	54	48	192	54,000	6,600
Guards—1st, 2nd, 3rd, 4th, 5th, 6th, 7th, 8th, 11th, 12th Corps on the Rhine	302	256	1,056	302,000	35,200
South German troops — Baden, Würtemburg, Bavaria	93	68	288	87,000	9,300
Total on the Rhine and Southern Germany ..	395	324	1,344	389,000	44,500
				433,500	

In order to make these figures nearly tally with my previous ones I should remind my readers that the Engineers' train is not included in the above totals; and that in my own figures I allowed for the feeding reserve of 220 guns, 129,000 infantry, and 16,000 cavalry, all close by in the fortresses and camps, and available at any moment, since they could be replaced, as they afterwards were, by the *Landwehr*.

The German armies were commanded by the King of Prussia, who had General von Moltke as his strategical director; Lieutenant-General von Blumenthal was Chief of the Crown Prince of Prussia's staff; while Colonel von Stiehle held a similar position on the staff of Prince Frederick Charles.

The Emperor Napoleon commanded the French army in person, with Marshal Leboeuf as his Chief of the staff, or *Majeur-Général de l'Armée*.

The position of the French advanced corps was well suited for attack, but not at all adapted for defence, as they covered such an extent of front. Assuming the offensive, they might have cut the rails and held the junction of the lines from Trèves (Trier), Bingen, and Mayence, and thereby have severed the communications of the different German armies with each other, besides ascertaining the arrival of the enemy in great force at Trèves and at Landau; at which latter the Crown Prince massed large bodies of his troops quite close to the division of General Felix Douay, who appears to have been totally unaware of his vicinity. In fact, the French seem to have thought that the Germans would act entirely on the defensive, and this may in some measure account for the gross carelessness and inactivity of their leaders.

The German commanders advanced rapidly to the positions assigned to them, and their armies were complete in materiel of every kind. Finding the French still inactive, the Germans taking the initiative assumed the offensive, and advanced to the frontier; and on the 4th of August the Crown Prince of Prussia struck the first effective blow of the campaign.

Having thus given the positions of the two armies at the commencement of the campaign, I shall restrict my narrative to the events more immediately affecting the Battle of Sedan.

War is considered to have been declared on the 15th July, 1870, when M. Ollivier made his memorable speech in the *Corps Législatif*, though the formal declaration was delayed a few days.

The causes of this great war between two neighbouring and powerful nations lie out of my province and find no place here, as my object is merely to give a rough and general sketch of the Battle of Sedan, to enable my readers to understand more clearly, and if I succeed in doing that, my object will be achieved.

Before the first action took place, the following changes had been effected in the disposition of the French army:—

The Imperial Guard had reached Metz, the 6th Corps had arrived at Nancy, and the 1st was between Strasbourg and the Lauter.

On the 21st July a skirmish took place near Saarbrücken.

On the 2nd August, the heights of Saarbrücken were carried by the French.

On the 4th, a portion of Marshal MacMahon's corps, under General Abel Douay, was defeated and routed at Weissenbourg by the Crown Prince of Prussia, and its commander killed.

On the 6th, the forces under Marshal MacMahon were totally defeated at Wörth by the Crown Prince of Prussia, and General Froissard's corps was beaten at Spicheren and driven back on Metz by General von Steinmetz's army.

On the 10th, Bazaine's, Canrobert's, Froissard's, and L'Admirault's corps and the Imperial Guard concentrated at Metz under Marshal Bazaine.

On the 14th, the indecisive action at Courcelles was fought.

On the 16th, Bazaine was beaten back from Mars la Tour.

On the 18th, the bloody and decisive battle of Gravelotte was fought, and Bazaine's army driven back on Metz.

The Lines of the Saar, Moselle, and Meuse, and the Passes of the Vosges, being abandoned, and Bazaine surrounded at Metz, I shall now follow the fortunes of MacMahon, who had retreated to the camp at Châlons with the remnant of his shattered army, and had there been organizing the levies of *Garde Mobile*, and shall continue to narrate the movements of the forces under him up to the final catastrophe around Sedan.

The political situation was as follows:— On the 9th August the Ollivier Ministry resigned, and on the following day Count Palikao assumed the reins of the Government by command of the Emperor, who also on the 17th appointed General Trochu—famous for a work (published in 1867) advocating an immediate reform in the army—to be Governor of Paris, and Commander-in-Chief of the forces assembling for its defence.

On the 19th, the Empress Regent issued a decree, appointing a Defence Committee for Paris, constituted as follows:—General Trochu, President; Admiral Rigault de Genouilly, Baron Jerome David, Marshal Vaillant, Generals de Chaubaud la Tour, Guiod, d'Autemarre, d'Erville, and Soumain, Members; and a number of defensive works were commenced to complete the circle of forts surrounding the capital.

Meanwhile MacMahon having retreated through Saverne, had been collecting the remnant of his corps at Châlons, and had under his command about 140,000 men belonging to the corps of De Failly, Felix Douay, and Canrobert. He had also about 36,000 *Garde Mobile*, recently levied, and with so little discipline as to be almost a hindrance to his future movements. Their want of discipline had, in fact, infected the old soldiers, previously disposed to be insubordinate from their disorderly and hasty retreat, and from a want of confidence in their leaders, who had shown such culpable incapacity in the opening engagements of the campaign.

Irregularities and disorderly conduct prevailed in his camp, instead of the stern discipline and constant drill so necessary to bring his discouraged troops and raw levies to that standard of excellence which alone could have saved him from the final disaster to which he was rapidly drifting.

The troops spent their time in the baneful delirium of the concert rooms, and dancing saloons, and all the worst features of a large garrison town prevailed; while not a few publicly abused the Emperor and their own commanders, without any restraint being placed upon them, or any steps being taken to check the rapidly rising symptoms of insubordination.

Such was the state of things when the Emperor arrived at Mac-

Mahon's Headquarters, having but narrowly escaped the ubiquitous Germans in his retreat from Metz.

There were two plans that then recommended themselves to the Emperor and MacMahon: one was to retreat towards Paris, harassing, if possible, the flank of the Crown Prince of Prussia's army; and the other was to attack the rear of the German armies investing Metz, and so, relieving Bazaine, possibly annihilate that portion of the enemy's forces, and catch the Crown Prince between the reunited French armies and the Army of Paris.

A council of war was held in the camp, and it was thereat determined to pursue the former course, and retreat on Paris, as the latter was considered too dangerous an experiment with the troops available, and with so determined and active an opponent as the Crown Prince.

The folly of the movements of an army in the field being directed, principally for political reasons, from the capital, instead of by those on the spot, able to judge, better than those at a distance, of the dispositions of the enemy, and of the materials they themselves have at their command, was now fully and unfortunately evinced.

The Empress Regent and the Ministry of Count Palikao directed MacMahon to proceed to the relief of Metz, and on no account to retreat on Paris, pointing out the danger the Emperor would incur should he return to the capital leaving Bazaine shut in around Metz.

MacMahon at first remonstrated, and breaking up the camp at Châlons, commenced on the 21st his march to Rheims, intending to retreat on Paris; writing at the same time to the Government, that it was necessary to rest and reorganize his army under the protection of the Paris forts, ere he could hope to offer any successful resistance to the rapidly advancing enemy.

He foresaw the extreme danger, so evident to the military student, of a flank march across a difficult country in such close proximity to so enterprising an enemy acting on interior lines. At all times, and under the most favourable circumstances, such a march would be made with imminent risk; but in face of an enemy so active in his movements, so superior in point of numbers, with troops elated by recent successes, and with the knowledge of the inferiority of the morale and equipment of his own troops, MacMahon, though but a poor strategist at any time, saw the risk he would ran, and felt the serious responsibility of giving in to the wishes of the Government, and of making the attempt.

Bois de la Folizette

Fleigneux

9. Division

St. Mengea

Etang St. Bar
Vrigne aux Bois

Iges

XI.
Arm.-K.

Floing

Bruncourt

Marancourt

4. Kav. Div.

Gaulier

Cazal

Villette

Can. de derivation

Glaire

le Dancourt

Württemb. Div.

Meuse

Maas

Torcy
Stat.

Bockbr.
V. Korps
d. XI.

Donchery

Bellevue

Pet. Torcy

SEDAN

183 m

Frenois

Wadelincourt

d. II. bayr. A. K.

6. B

Ulanen Brig.

Standpunkt
d. Kön. v. Preußen

112 m

Bois de
La Marfée

le Pont Man

Noyers

Chaumont St. Quentin

Stellung d. beiden Armeen
Mittags 12 Uhr.
Deutsche
Franzosen
Infant. Kav. Artillerie
Maßstab 1: 115 000
Kilometer

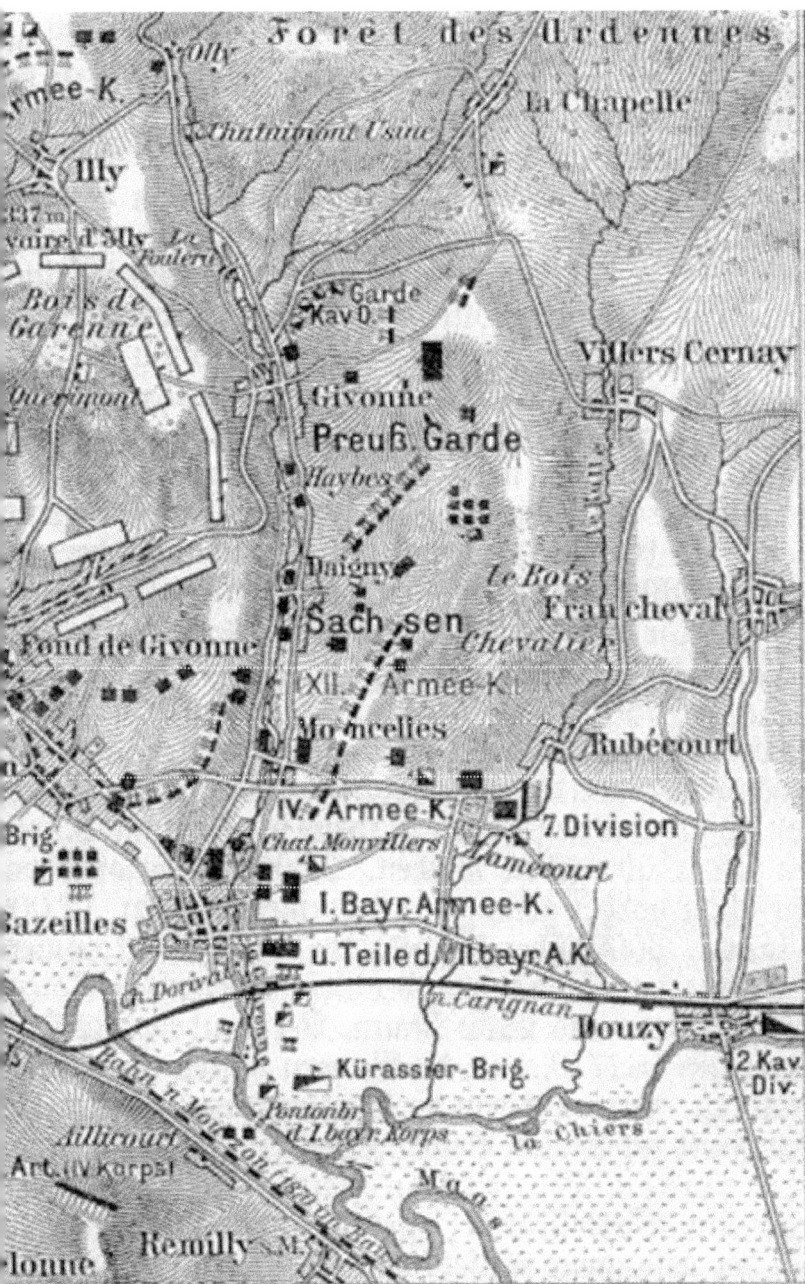

Forêt des Ardennes

Olly

La Chapelle

Armée-K.

Illy

Chatuimont Usine

437 m

voire d'Illy

Le Fouleru

Bois de Garenne

Garde
Kav D.

Villers Cernay

Guérimont

Givonne

Preuß. Garde

Haybes

Daigny

Le Bois

Francheval

Chevalier

Fond de Givonne

Sach sen

XII. Armée-K.

Moncelles

Rubécourt

IV. Armée-K.

Brig.

Chat. Monvillers

Fumécourt

7. Division

Bazeilles

I. Bayr. Armée-K.

u. Teil d. II. bayr. A. K.

Ch. Dorival

Bahn n. Mon

n. Carignan

Douzy

Kürassier-Brig.

2. Kav. Div.

Le Chiers

Pontonbr.
d. I. bayr. Korps

Aillicourt

Art. (IV. Korps)

La Meuse

lonne

Remilly M.

That the Emperor also held the same views we now know from the contents of a pamphlet, since published at Brussels, purporting to be from the pen of one of the Imperial Headquarter Staff, but attributed to the Emperor, or written at his instigation, and there is but little doubt that its contents may be considered authentic.

The Emperor had at first wished to resume the reins of power in Paris, but had yielded to the wishes of the Regency that he would not do so.

He dissented, however, from the course proposed by the Empress Regent and the Government; as from his knowledge, gained in the field, of the position, numbers, and resources of the Germans, and seeing the condition of his own troops, he felt convinced that the proposed flank march was pregnant with dangers innumerable. Unfortunately, however, he failed to put his veto on the move, from what may now be considered a false notion, that he had no longer any right to interfere with the plans of those to whom after all he had only temporarily entrusted the Imperial power.

Had he used his authority to prevent the fatal flank march, the history of the campaign might have been very different; but he wavered, hesitated, and then resigned himself to his fate, showing again that fatal indecision and want of firmness which had characterized all his movements from the commencement of the campaign; and one can only attribute to sickness of body the want of *élan* and firmness that had previously been his *métier*.

Feeble in body, and borne down by the unexpected calamities that had so suddenly overtaken him, his mind wanted vigour, and accompanied by his son, thus early taught (poor child!) his first lesson in the rough school of adversity, and oppressed with anxiety for the fixture of his dynasty, the feeling of whose coming downfall already overshadowed him, he hampered the movements of the Marshal and his army, to whom his safety was an hourly anxiety, and carried with him, amidst his disheartened soldiers, not the martial presence (inspiring confidence) of the First Empire, but the idle pomp and state of the third, utterly out of place on such an occasion.

His carriages, horses, escorts, and baggage waggons blocked the road, and impeded the onward march, while the daily necessities of his numerous retinue trenched largely on the resources of the ill-managed *Intendance*.

Fallen greatness is always the object of our deepest sympathies, and no one more than myself feels for the Emperor, deserted in his hour of need by those who but yesterday hypocritically fawned upon him, and received (cap in hand) the favours he lavished on all but himself; and I trust I may not be deemed presumptuous in expressing the hope that he may soon again have it in his power to restore France to the high and prosperous position she so long maintained under the Imperial sway; but I cannot conclude this digression without giving it as my opinion that had the Emperor gone through the campaign, after the first reverses as a general, without the pomp of a sovereign, and shared more jealously the privations of his soldiers, not one but would have followed him cheerfully into his temporary captivity with feelings of devotion and respect.

The Government in Paris, wishing to encourage the Parisians with the hope that Bazaine could be released from Metz, and backed by the Privy Council, now issued imperative orders to MacMahon to advance to the relief of Metz, and by forced marches to traverse the passes of the Argonne, and crossing the Meuse, to operate from the line of Montmédy, Longuyon, and Thionville, against the rear of the German army investing Metz.

The language of reason was no longer understood in Paris, and MacMahon, yielding to the pressure put upon him by the Government, and fearing his objection to march to the relief of Bazaine might be attributed to personal jealousy, quitted Rheims with his army on the 22nd August, and marched towards Bethenville, on the Suippe, but his rear-guard did not clear Rheims till the following day.

The forces under the Marshal were composed of the remnant of his own 1st Corps (all veterans, of African experiences); of the 5th Corps, under De Failly; of the 7th Corps, under General Felix Douay; of the 12th Corps, composed of new regiments of reserve troops, and of marines; and of a portion of the cavalry of Canrobert's corps. Besides these he had about 500 field-pieces and *mitrailleuses*.

The soldiers were more or less disaffected, and the disgraceful plundering that took place on the departure of the army from Rheims, showed the utter want of discipline prevailing; in fact, the new levies were rather a source of weakness than of strength to the Marshal, as they straggled, and could not be persuaded to march at a fair pace; a most important point, when, we consider the necessity there was for forced marches, if the enemy were to be successfully eluded.

The *Intendance* broke down immediately after starting, and MacMahon was forced to diverge in his march, so as to move along the line of railway; and he reached Rethel on the 24th, whither he had directed his route, in order to obtain the necessary supplies for his troops, which were being hurried on by the railway from Mézières to Thionville, while the line was also employed to bring up reinforcements in the shape of new levies. His cavalry, and the larger portion of his guns, had, however, been sent on in advance towards Montmédy, by Suippe and Vouziers.

Meanwhile the Germans were rapidly advancing north-eastwards, and feeling their way all over the country; and such was the terror of the peasantry, that the presence of three or four *Uhlans* (German Lancers) was sufficient to cause a panic in a village, and all classes seemed paralyzed.

The main body of Prince Frederick Charles's army were surrounding Bazaine's army in and around Metz, and having entrenched themselves strongly, by the 23rd they had completed the investing circle.

The Crown Prince of Prussia was pushing forward towards Paris, and his advance guard reached the deserted Châlons on the 24th August. He was supported on his right by a portion of Prince Frederick Charles's army, about 80,000 strong, consisting of the 4th Corps, the 12th Saxons, and of the Prussian Guards under the command of the Crown Prince of Saxony, who swept the country along the Belgian frontier northwards, keeping parallel with the Crown Prince, and marching by Verdun and Menehould.

The King of Prussia arrived on the 24th August at Ligny, where the Headquarters of the Crown Prince were established.

On the 25th the Crown Prince reached Bar-le-Duc, when his advanced guard sent him the news that MacMahon had broken up his camp at Châlons, burnt his tents, and marching through Rheims, had struck off in a northerly direction.

According to Count Moltke's instructions the Crown Prince of Saxony was immediately directed to oppose MacMahon's march, and keep him in check, while the Crown Prince was to sweep round on his right flank, and throw him back on to the Belgian frontier.

On the 26th the Crown Prince of Saxony was marching for Stenay on the Meuse, and the Crown Prince of Prussia was hurrying the 3rd Army on by forced marches to Clermont-en-Argonne and Grand Pré.

Meanwhile MacMahon had been advancing but slowly, whereas the only chance of success on his part lay in the rapidity of his movements, as, having a good start of the Crown Prince of Prussia, he might have engaged the Crown Prince of Saxony alone had he pushed on quickly, and, driving him back towards Metz, have enabled Bazaine to break the circle of investment, and thus have united the two French armies. But his heart was not in the march, and his troops were influenced by his slowness.

The Marshal had divided his army into three divisions; one of which, consisting of 20,000 men, proceeded by rail to Mézières, where it was to join a corps from Paris under General Vinoy, and to follow the other divisions as soon as they should have effected the passage of the Meuse. The other two divisions under MacMahon himself moved by two roads; one to the north by Stonne and Mouzon, the other to the south by Vouziers and Buzancy, both heading for Montmddy.

On the 27th, on reaching Le Chêne Populeux, MacMahon first ascertained the immediate danger of his position, and the near approach of the German armies. His first impulse was to retreat, and indeed he gave orders to that effect, but the Government again sent him orders to advance, and he yielded himself up to the necessity of carrying them out.

On the same date some Prussian outposts were driven back by the French near Vouziers; and at Buzancy the 12th Regiment of French Chasseurs was dispersed and fearfully cut up by the 3rd Cavalry, some of the 18th Uhlans, and a battery of Prussian guns.

On the 28th, the outposts were engaged at Dun, Stenay, and Mouzon; and Vouziers, an important junction of roads through the Argonnes, fell into German hands.

On the 29th, the village of Vrizy, occupied by *Turcos*, was taken by two squadrons of Prussian Hussars, and two officers of MacMahon's staff were taken into Grand Pré as prisoners by some *Uhlans*.

By the same date the Crown Prince of Saxony was in possession of both sides of the Meuse at Stenay, while the Crown Prince of Prussia was nearing the French right advance; thus MacMahon was threatened in flank and rear, his army being concentrated behind Stonne and Mouzon preparing to cross the Meuse, while he himself had his Headquarters at Raucourt.

By this time he was fully aware of the peril of his position, and that the Crown Prince of Saxony was prepared to dispute his further advance towards Metz; while the probability of the Crown Prince of Prussia having turned off from his march on Paris, and being on his way to assist the Crown Prince of Saxony, necessitated his crossing the Meuse early next morning, and beating back the combined army without further loss of time.

BRIDGE BLOWN UP BY THE FRENCH

In despair, he felt the necessity of immediately playing his last card, and of trying to force the Germans back to the Moselle, feeling sure that, if defeated, he could retreat on Sedan and Mézières, and there holding his antagonists in check, delay their onward march to Paris till the National Guards and other levies should be ready for its defence. Meanwhile, he was hourly expecting stores and reinforcements of the 13th Corps, such as they might be, by the Northern railways of France, by way of St. Quentin, Avernes, and Hirson, and he considered that the proximity of the Belgian frontier would make any attempt to turn his left flank futile.

Although his orders were peremptory, and counselled haste, still his slowness in carrying them out, on which doubtless the Government at Paris had not calculated, and the ignorance of strategy he as usual displayed, must, I think, to a certain extent condemn his movements in any history of the war. He had thrown away the position that promised most hope of success, namely, the line between Rethel and Mézières, whence, if beaten, he could have retreated to Laon and Soissons, and his retreat to Paris would probably have still been feasible; whereas his present line of retreat could only be by Mézières and Sedan, if the Crown Prince of Prussia should remain ignorant of his movements, a hope which that commander's former proceedings by no means justified; or else through a corner of Belgium, in which case he would infringe its neutrality, and bring political complications on France which she was ill prepared to grapple with.

And here I think a sketch of the life and previous career of Marshal MacMahon will not be out of place. His name is Marie Edme Patrick Maurice MacMahon, and he is a descendant of a noble Celtic family, whose members fought in Ireland for the last of the Stuarts, and afterwards emigrated to France. He was born at the Chateau de Sully, near Autun, in the year 1808, and was educated at the seminary of that town. At seventeen he went to the military school of St. Cyr, and leaving it after two years with the rank of "*sous-lieutenant élève*," he joined the Staff School of Application.

He acted in Algeria in 1830 as orderly officer to General Achard, and distinguished himself in the first Medeah expedition, by carrying an important despatch through the Arabian army to Blidah. For this he received the cross of the Legion of Honour. In 1832 he was present at the siege of Antwerp, where he was promoted to the rank of captain. In 1836, at the second siege of Constantine, in Algeria, he acted as *aide-de-camp* to General Damrémont, and being wounded, he received the rank of Officer of the Legion of Honour. Next we find him on the staff of General Changarnier, and in 1841 he was appointed to command a regiment of *Chasseurs-à-pied,* and assisted later in subduing the great Arab chief, Abd-el-Kader. In 1855 he replaced General Canrobert in the command of the 1st Division of the French Crimean army, and directed the attack on the Malakoff. In 1856 he became a senator. In 1857 and 1858 he commanded the Algerian forces. In 1859 he was engaged in the Italian campaign; on the 3rd June he gained a victory at Turbigo, and on the 4th turned the battle of Magenta into a victory for the arms of France.

For this latter he was made a Marshal of France, and received the title of Duke of Magenta on the field of battle. In 1861 he went to Berlin as ambassador extraordinary. Shortly afterwards he was appointed Governor-General of Algeria. He also, for a season, commanded one of the summer camps of instruction at Châlons. He was always noted for his energy and personal courage, and made a splendid General of Division; but no event has yet shown his fitness to command an army, while his recent defeats have rather proved the contrary.

Early on the morning of the 30th, the French began to cross the Meuse, and Paris was cheered by the news, telegraphed by the Emperor, that two corps of MacMahon's army, having crossed in safety, were marching on Montmédy by way of Carignan, at which place he himself afterwards was present, during its occupation by the troops.

These two corps alluded to proceeded through Vaux to Carignan.

Hardly had they effected the passage of the river in safety, when the right wing, under De Failly, which was encamped north of Beaumont, and which had been thrown back facing south to cover the flank and rear of MacMahon's army during its passage of the Meuse, was surprised by the 1st Bavarian corps of the 3rd Army (Crown Prince of Prussia), which, apprised by its scouts of the presence of the enemy in its front, had under cover of the intervening woods advanced, and catching De Failly's corps unawares, routed it with severe loss; the tents, camp equipage, large quantities of baggage, and numerous prisoners falling into the victors' hands.

The 4th Prussian corps, forming the left of the combined army (Crown Prince of Saxony), was simultaneously advancing up the Meuse, and to the right of the 1st Bavarian corps.

The 5th Prussian corps was moving on Stonne, while the 11th was making for Chemery; and the 2nd Bavarians were supporting the advance.

MARSHAL MACMAHON

The artillery cannonade above Beaumont had no sooner commenced, than the different advanced posts pushing forwards opened fire, and a general fusillade ensued.

De Failly's corps being routed, and his flank and rear exposed, MacMahon immediately ordered the troops on the west bank of the Meuse to retreat across the river, masking the move with great tactical skill, and the French fought gallantly on this occasion; but only a portion of them had reached the opposite bank, when the 4th Corps, forming the left of the combined army, sweeping up the eastern bank from Stenay, and forming line, fell upon the French, already in great confusion from their hurried retreat at Mouzon, and utterly routed them with heavy loss.

About the same time the two French corps, which had crossed early in the day, and whose advance had already entered Carignan, were attacked by the 12th Corps of the combined army, supported by the Prussian Guards, and driven back across a small river called the Chiers, which runs north-west from Carignan, and empties itself into the Meuse near Remilly, and behind which they effected a junction with the remainder of MacMahon's army, which had evacuated Stonne and all its advanced posts, and fallen back along the eastern banks of the Meuse; so great indeed was the panic of the centre, that the troops threw away their arms and accoutrements, and the whole French army crossed the Chiers before the panic could in any way be checked, or any attempt at a more orderly retreat be made.

Night coming to their aid, found the French army behind the Chiers, between Douzy and Remilly; while the combined German army, and the 1st Bavarian corps of the 3rd Army, bivouacked on the ground that they had won,—the 4th Corps having taken several thousand prisoners and twelve cannon; the 12th, numerous prisoners and four *mitrailleuses*; and the 1st Bavarian corps, several prisoners, a few cannon, large quantities of baggage, and stores of different kinds.

The total French losses were estimated at 7,000 prisoners, besides the killed and wounded, and 20 guns. The result of the day was to stop MacMahon's advance to the south-east.

The main body of the 3rd Army, acting under instructions from General Moltke, which were carried out by its commander and General Blumenthal (Chief of his staff), had been engaged since the 26th in swinging round half-right on to the French line, and in performing a sort of right wheel on an extended circle, in order to throw back MacMahon's right, and cut him off from any retreat, unless he should choose to infringe the neutrality of Belgium. The positions of the corps in this strategical movement were similar to those shown on the small plan; and only one corps, the 6th, having the outer or most westerly portion of the circle to march on, was unable to arrive in time to take part in the engagements that led up to, and concluded in, the Battle of Sedan; it marched, however, to its point diagonally, and was ready to guard the German left and to support the Würtemburgers if necessary.

Opposed to an active enemy commanding a well-organized army, this would have been a most dangerous manoeuvre, as the German rear might have been attacked while the armies occupied so extended a line; but shrewdly guessing at the condition of his enemy's troops, and not believing in any such danger, the Crown Prince of Prussia swung his left round, and by the dogged pluck of his troops throughout the forced marches, which were necessarily of the most fatiguing nature, succeeded in carrying out the strategical movement ordered by General Moltke; and in a great measure to the endurance and splendid marching of the 5th and 11th Corps, who had nearly the outer edge of the circle to traverse, and who marched twenty-five miles on the 30th, must be attributed the German success at Sedan.

During the 30th, with the exception of its right corps, the 1st Bavarians, who bore the brunt of the day so nobly, the troops of the 3rd Army were hardly engaged, except in trifling outpost skirmishes, as neither party was near each other in force; and the evening found them, wearied with their severe marches, occupying Beaumont, and bivouacking about Stonne and the country on either side of it.

The campfires, extending along a line from near Chemery, through Stonne, Beaumont, Mouzon, and Carignan, showed during the night of the 30th the positions held by the two German armies.

During the day the King of Prussia had sent the following telegram to the Queen at Berlin:—

Varennes, August 30th, 3.30 p.m.—We won a victorious battle yesterday. MacMahon was beaten by the 4th and 12th Saxon and the 1st Bavarian Army corps, and was driven back from Beaumont beyond the Meuse, near Mouzon. Twelve cannon and several thousand prisoners, together with a very large quantity of war *matériel*, are in our hands. Our losses are moderate. I am about to return to the battlefield, to follow up the results of the victory. May God help us further in His mercy, as He has

PRUSSIAN SOLDIERS

done hitherto.

During the 31st, both French and German commanders were making their dispositions for the supreme effort, and some desultory fighting took place between Douzy and Bazeilles.

The following telegram was also sent officially to Germany:—

Varennes, August 31st—The results of yesterday's victory over Marshal MacMahon's army only become known gradually, in consequence of the great extent of the battle-field. Up to the present it is ascertained that some 20 cannons, 11 *mitrailleurs*, and about 7,000 prisoners have fallen into our hands.

The German plan for the next day arranged by Moltke was as follows: the combined army (4th) was to advance before nightfall, and occupy a new line on the Chiers; at the same time the 3rd Army was to occupy a position to a certain extent along the Meuse, and extending from Remilly on the right to Donchéry on the left. On the following morning (1st September) they were to engage the enemy at daybreak; the Crown Prince of Saxony was to cross the Chiers, and attacking the French in front, as soon as possible wheel round his right flank, turn their left, detaching a force from his extreme right to sweep round near the Belgian frontier under the cover of the woods, and effect a junction north-east of Sedan with a detachment of the 3rd Army, sent round by the Crown Prince of Prussia, who would simultaneously engage the right centre of MacMahon's army at Bazeilles, and endeavour to overwhelm his right wing; when, if both the German armies should prove successful, the French army would be enveloped, and being hemmed in at Sedan, would have to surrender unconditionally. How ably and gallantly this plan was carried out in every particular is now a matter of history.

During the whole of the 31st the Germans were taking up the positions assigned to them, and marched along in review order, their knapsacks being carried on country carts and ambulances; the King of Prussia slept at Vendresse; the Crown Prince of Saxony moved his Headquarters to Villers-lez-Mouzon, and his right, consisting of the Prussian Guards, occupied the heights above Francheval. The Crown Prince of Prussia advanced his Headquarters to Chehery, though most of the correspondents named Chemery as his Headquarters, a place about three miles south of the former, to which similarity of names doubtless the mistake may be attributed. About 4 a.m. on the morning of the 1st September the German armies were, as nearly as can at present be ascertained, in the positions ascribed to them in the small plan.

MacMahon might have escaped with the greater portion of his army by rapid marching on the 31st, in the direction of Mézières, had he abandoned his baggage and such artillery as was not efficiently horsed; but he feared to risk a running fight with his disheartened troops, and preferred offering battle to the enemy in the following position, which he took up, evidently expecting to be attacked in front and on the right flank; and which position both the Emperor and himself seem to have thought offered a fair chance of success.

His left rested on Givonne; and he considered his position in its vicinity so strong, from the heights surrounding it intersected by ravines and broken ground, and covered with dense forests, that he placed there his weakest troops, evidently believing that the natural obstacles and the proximity of the Belgian frontier would prevent his left flank being turned, or even seriously attacked. Thence his line extended to the Meuse by Balan, and Bazeilles, the key to his right centre, and which latter, from its being on the high road to Carignan and projecting rather beyond his line, he occupied in great force with his best troops; entrenching this line where he deemed it advisable, and placing his guns on such wooded eminences as he thought would best cover them, and enable them to catch the enemy at a disadvantage in the intervening valleys. His right was drawn up north of Sedan, protected by the Meuse and the western end of the fortress and town, and by the system of artificial inundations previously mentioned, and held the village of St. Menges and the plateaux and ridges of Floing and La Garenne.

Looking at all the circumstances of the case, and taking into consideration his determination not to retreat without engaging the enemy, this was probably the best position he could have chosen. His line from Givonne to Bazeilles, on a series of wooded heights, intersected by three parallel ravines, running north and south from the Belgian frontier, two towards the Chiers, and the third close to Sedan towards the Meuse, with the Chiers between him and the bulk of the right of his enemy, formed a succession of formidable lines of defence; while the eminences near Floing and La Garenne, crowned with woods and villages, every one of which might be successively defended, with the Meuse, forming a double obstacle to be overcome by the Germans, made his right flank, as he thought, almost unassailable.

The strength of the position he thus took up does not in my opinion absolve the Marshal from the flagrant error in strategical judgment he undoubtedly committed in not retreating towards Mézières, and trying to engage and defeat the 3rd Army before the combined army could come to its assistance; and he had still possession of the railway to aid him in the attempt, had he essayed this early on the 31st. But having determined to fight in the positions he took up, I conceive his chief faults were:

1st, not having strong cavalry patrols along the road to the Belgian frontier,

2nd, not ascertaining more correctly the movements of the 3rd Army approaching his right; and

3rd, in not destroying the railway bridge across the Meuse near Bazeilles, by means of which the 1st Bavarians chiefly crossed; and this latter is the more unaccountable as the other railway bridge at Villette was blown up by his orders. Further criticism on his movements I leave to the future historians of the campaign.

As far as can be at present ascertained, the number of the French troops engaged on the 1st of September was about 100,000, divided into four corps, and commanded as follows:—

1st Corps	General Ducrot,
5th "	General De Wimpffen,
7th "	General Douay,
12th "	General Lebrun,

with about 450 guns and *mitrailleuses*. Marshal MacMahon commanded in chief, while the Emperor was present, but without any definite command until the battle ceased.

Besides the above, one division of the French marched from Mézières to join in the battle, but after a short skirmish with the Würtemburgers retreated to that fortress.

The Germans were about 200,000 strong; for although General Moltke originally computed them at 240,000, yet we must remember that the 6th Corps took no part in the battle, and the 4th Corps was only partially engaged, and that after the hardest portion of the action was finished. The King commanded in person; while the 3rd Army, composed of the 1st and 2nd Bavarian corps, the Würtemburger division, and the 5th and 11th Corps, besides a large force of cavalry, was under the Crown Prince of Prussia; and the 4th or combined army,

FRENCH SOLDIERS

consisting of the 4th and 12th Corps and of the Prussian Guards (the 4th Grenadier regiment of which lost 500 men out of a thousand), was under the Crown Prince of Saxony. From 600 to 700 guns were divided amongst these two armies.

On the King of Prussia's staff were, amongst others, Generals von Moltke and von Roon, and Count Bismarck; Generals Sheridan and Forsyth, of the United States army; and the correspondent of the *Pall Mall Gazette*.

Accompanying the Crown Prince of Prussia were the Dukes of Augustenberg and Coburg Gotha, and the Princes of Weimar, Mecklenburg, Würtemburg, and Hohenzollern, and the correspondent of the *Daily News*.

Early on the morning of the 1st the French and German armies were nearly in the positions shown in the small plan, and under cover of a thick fog the combined army crossed the Chiers in safety unperceived, and the 1st Bavarian corps made the passage of the Meuse unopposed, partly by the railway bridge and partly on pontoons; and effecting a junction with the left of the combined army, advanced to the attack of Bazeilles.

At the same time the 5th and 11th Corps of the 3rd Army were marching northwards to get round the bend of the Meuse, and then attack St. Menges and the troops in position behind Floing and the woods of La Garenne. The cavalry under Count Stolberg were massed west of the Meuse, under cover of some hills, and out of cannon-shot range; and the 2nd Bavarian corps was advancing to occupy the commanding hills south of Sedan and of the Meuse, accompanied by a powerful artillery.

The King of Prussia and his staff took up a position on a hill above the village of Cheveuge; and the Crown Prince of Prussia on an eminence half a mile off to the west, in front of a newly-built *château* overlooking Donchéry, in which respective positions both remained nearly the whole day.

Before 6 a.m., only a few shots were fired, but the fog lifting about that hour, the Bavarians commenced a heavy cannonade, and the sun shone down mockingly on the effects of man's ambition below.

To describe the battle with the meagre details at command is beyond my pen, but I subjoin the general features of it, and trust they may enable my readers to form some idea of the principal tactics on both sides, which resulted in the overthrow of the French under the walls of Sedan.

Soon after 6 a.m. the action became general, and the 11th Corps forced its way into St. Menges, under cover of a heavy Prussian cannonade from a battery splendidly served posted on ground commanding the village of Floing; and the 5th Corps slowly but gradually crept round through Fleigneux and Illy, northwest of Sedan.

The 2nd Bavarians meanwhile were throwing quantities of concussion shells into the troops defending Balan and Bazeilles, already on fire in several places, and which latter the 1st Bavarians were attacking gallantly in front, while it was as gallantly defended, principally by marines, and a very serious fight ensued for its possession.

The 4th German corps was rapidly coming up in support, while the 12th Corps to the right was attacking the defenders of the line of Givonne, Daigny, and La Moncelle. Behind this latter corps, in reserve, were the Prussian Guards, covering the road to Carignan and Montmédy.

Soon after nine a heavy artillery fire was going forward along the whole attack, and the French left near Givonne was turned by the combined army, and beaten back panic-stricken into the woods, and the Germans pushed their right rapidly round in a northwesterly direction.

By this time, however, the 1st Bavarians and 12th Saxons were undergoing a very heavy fire of musketry and *mitrailleuses*, and shortly before eleven the grunt of the latter, and the sharp rattle of the former became one continued roll, showing how well the French appreciated the importance of holding Bazeilles.

On the German left the battery near Floing had silenced two French batteries opposed to it, and, no longer supported by their guns, the infantry evacuated Floing, and soon after were forced to retreat still nearer to Sedan, owing to the numberless effective shells which burst amongst their ranks, pitched by a Prussian battery at St. Menges.

At twelve noon the long-desired junction was effected between the Crown Prince of Prussia's left and the Crown Prince of Saxony's right, and from that moment the result of the day could no longer be in doubt; and though numberless moves of troops were subsequently made, every change was limited to so confined a space as not to be worthy of being chronicled.

Soon after this, some of the French began to retreat from Bazeilles, while others were going to support its defenders through the woods of La Garenne. At one o'clock the 11th Corps advanced to take the hill north-west of La Garenne, and was received by a heavy artillery fire from the French batteries on the edge of the wood.

Describing the attack at this position of the line, and what followed, the correspondent of the *Pall Mall Gazette* writes:—

At 1.5 yet another French battery near the wood opened on the Prussian columns, which were compelled to keep shifting their ground till ready for their final rush at the hill, in order to avoid offering so good a mark to the French shells. Shortly after we saw the first Prussian skirmishers on the crest of the La Garenne hill above Torcy. They did not seem in strength, and General Sheridan standing beside me exclaimed, 'Ah! the beggars are too weak, they can never hold that position against all those French.' The General's prophecy soon proved correct, for the French advancing at least six to one, the Prussians were forced to retire down the hill, to seek reinforcements from the columns which were hurrying to their support.

In five minutes they came back again, this time in greater force, but still terribly inferior to the huge French columns. 'Good heavens! the French *Cuirassiers* are going to charge them,' said General Sheridan; and sure enough the regiment of *Cuirassiers*, their helmets and breast-plates flashing in the September sun, form up in sections of squadrons, and dash down on the Prussian scattered skirmishers. Without deigning to form line—squares are never used by the Prussians—the infantry received the *Cuirassiers* with a most tremendous '*schnell-feuer*' (quick fire), at about 108 yards, loading and firing as fast as possible into the dense squadrons.

Over went men and horses by hundreds, and the regiment was compelled to retire much faster, it seemed to me, than it came. The moment the *Cuirassiers* turned bridle the plucky Prussians actually dashed in hot pursuit after them at the double. Such a thing has not often been recorded in the annals of war. The French infantry then came forward in turn and attacked the Prussians, who waited quietly under a most rapid firing of chassepots, until their enemies got within about 100 yards, when they gave them such a dose of lead that the infantry soon followed the cavalry to the 'place from which they came'—that is, behind a ridge some 600 yards on the way to Sedan, where the *tirailleurs* could not hit them.

The great object of the Prussians was gained, as they were not dispossessed of the crest of the hill, and it was fair betting that they would do all that in them lay to get some artillery up to help them before Napoleon III. was much nearer his deposition. 'There will be a h— of a fight for that crest,' says Sheridan, peering through his field-glass at the hill, which was not three miles from where we stood, with the full fire on it from behind us. At half-past one the French cavalry, this time I fancy a regiment of *Carabineers*, made another attempt to dislodge the Prussians, who were being reinforced every minute. But they met with the same fate as their brethren in the iron jackets, and were sent with heavy loss to the right-about, the Prussians taking advantage of their flight to advance their line a couple of hundred yards nearer the French infantry.

Suddenly they split into two bodies, leaving a break of a hundred yards in their line. We were not long in seeing the object of this movement, for the little white puffs from the crest behind the skirmishers, followed by a commotion in the dense French masses, show us that '*ces diables de Prussiens*' have contrived, Heaven only knows how, to get a couple of 4-pounders up the steep ground, and have opened on the French. Something must have at this point been very wrong with the French infantry, for instead of attacking the Prussians—whom they still outnumbered by at least two to one—they remained in column on the lull, seeing their only hope of retrieving the day vanishing from before their eyes, without stirring.

The cavalry then tried to do a little Balaklava business, but without the success of the immortal six hundred. We *took* the guns in the Balaklava valley. Down came the *Cuirassiers* once more, this time riding straight for the two field-pieces. But before they had got within 200 yards of the guns the Prussians formed line as if on parade, and, waiting till they were within fifty yards, gave them a volley which seemed to us to destroy almost the whole of the leading squadron, and so actually block up the way to the guns for the next ones following.

After this last charge, which was as complete a failure—although most gallantly conceived and executed—as the two preceding ones, the infantry fell back rapidly towards Sedan, and in an instant the whole hill was covered by swarms of Prussian *tirailleurs*, who appeared to rise from the ground. After the last desperate charge of the French cavalry. General Sheridan remarked to me,

A PRUSSIAN PRIVATE

'I never saw anything so reckless, so utterly foolish, as that last charge—it was sheer murder.'

The Prussians, after the French infantry fell back, advanced rapidly, so much so that the retreating squadrons of French cavalry turned suddenly round and charged desperately once again. But it was all no use. The days of breaking squares or even lines are over, and the 'thin blue line' soon stopped the Gallic onset. It was most extraordinary that the French had neither artillery nor *mitrailleurs*—especially these latter—on the hill to support their infantry. The position was a most important one, and certainly worth straining every nerve to defend. One thing was clear enough, that the French infantry, after once meeting the Prussians, declined to try conclusions with them again, and that the cavalry were trying to encourage them by their example. About two, more Prussian reinforcements came over the long-disputed hill between Torcy and Sedan, to reinforce the regiments already established there.

All the time that this great conflict was going on 'under Fritz's eyes' and those of your correspondent, another was proceeding, none the less severe, and as murderous for the Bavarians as the one I have attempted to describe was for the French. If there was a want of *mitrailleurs* on the hill above Torcy, there was certainly none in the Bazeilles ravine. On that side there was for more than an hour one continuous roar of musketry and *mitrailleurs*, and the Bavarian officers told me on the 2nd that the loss in their regiments was terrific, the *mitrailleurs* having made lanes in their columns. At 2.5 p.m. the French totally abandoned the hill between Torcy and Sedan, and fell back on the *faubourg* of Cazal, just outside the ramparts of the town. 'Now the battle is lost for the French,' says General Sheridan, to the great delight of the Prussian officers.

One would almost have fancied that the French had heard his words, for they had hardly been uttered before there was a lull in the firing all along the line, or rather circle, as it has now become. Count Bismarck took advantage of this to come and have a talk with his English and American friends. I was anxious to know what the Federal Chancellor had done about the threatened neutrality of Belgium, and my curiosity was soon gratified.

'I have told the Belgian Minister of War,' said Count Bismarck, 'that so long as the Belgian troops do their utmost to disarm any number of French soldiers who may cross the frontier, I will strictly respect the neutrality of Belgium; but if, on the contrary, the Belgians, either through negligence or inability, do not disarm and capture every man in French uniform who sets his foot in their country, we shall at once follow the enemy into neutral territory with our troops, considering that the French have been the first to violate the Belgian soil. I have been down to have a look at the Belgian troops near the frontier,' added Herr von Bismarck, 'and I confess they do not inspire me with a very high opinion of their martial ardour or discipline. Why, when they have their great-coats on one can see a great deal of *paletôt*, but hardly any soldier.' I asked his Excellency whether he thought the Emperor was in Sedan. 'Oh, no,' was the reply, 'Napoleon is not very wise, but he is not quite so foolish as to put himself in Sedan just now.' For once in his life Count Bismarck was wrong.

At 2.45 the King came by where I was standing, saying he thought the French were going to try and break out just beneath us, in front of the 2nd Bavarian corps. At ten minutes to four General Sheridan told me that Napoleon and 'Loulu' were in Sedan. No one, however, believed this.

At 3.20 the Bavarians below us not only continue to get inside the fortifications of Sedan, but maintain themselves there, wending their way forward from house to house.

About four there was a great fight for the possession of the ridge above Bazeilles. That gone, Sedan was swept on all sides by the Prussian cannon. This point of vantage was carried by the Prussians at 4.40, and from that moment there could not be a shade of doubt as to the ultimate fate of Sedan.

Dr. Russell, writing to *The Times*, vividly describes the same scene, as well as the fighting at Bazeilles and Balan, in the following words:—

The Prussians coming up from Floing were invisible to me. Never can I forget the sort of agony with which I witnessed those who first came out on the plateau raising their heads and looking around for an enemy, while, hidden from view, a thick blue band of French infantry was awaiting them, and a brigade of cavalry was ready on their flank below. I did not know that Floing was filled with advancing columns. There was but a wide, extending, loose array of skirmishers, like a flock of rooks, on the plateau.

Now the men in front began to fire at the heads over the bank lined by the French. This drew such a flash of musketry as tumbled over some and staggered the others; but their comrades came scrambling up from the rear, when suddenly the first block of horse in the hollow shook itself up, and the line, in beautiful order, rushed up the slope. The onset was not to be withstood. The Prussians were caught *en flagrant délit* Those nearest the ridge slipped over into the declivitous ground; those in advance, running in vain, were swept away. But the impetuosity of the charge could not be stayed. Men and horses came tumbling down into the road, where they were disposed of by the Prussians in the gardens, while the troopers on the left of the line, who swept down the lane in a cloud of dust, were almost exterminated by the infantry in the village. There was also a regular cavalry encounter, I fancy, in the plains below, but I cannot tell at what time; the *Cuirassiers*, trying to cut their way out, were destroyed, and a change of two Prussian squadrons, which did not quite equal expectations, occurred.

The feat of these unfortunate cavaliers only cleared the plateau for a little time. In a few minutes up came the spiked helmets again over the French *épaulement*, crossing their sabred comrades, and therefore all alive to the danger of cavalry. They advanced in closer order, but still skirmishing, and one long, black parallelogram was maintained to rally on. As the skirmishers got to the ridge they began to fire, but the French in the second line of *épaulement* soon drove them back by a rattling fusillade. The French rushed out of the *épaulement* in pursuit, still firing. At the same moment a splendid charge was executed on the Prussians, before which the skirmishers rallied, on what seemed to me to be still a long parallelogram. They did not form square.

Some Prussians too far on were sabred. The troopers, brilliantly led, went right onwards in a cloud of dust; but when they were within a couple of hundred yards of the Prussians, one simultaneous volley burst out of the black front and flank, which enveloped all in smoke. They were steady soldiers who pulled trigger there. Down came horse and man; the array was utterly ruined. There was left in front of that deadly infantry but a heap of white and grey horses—a terrace of dead and dying and dismounted men and flying troopers, who tumbled at every instant. More total dissipation of a bright pageantry could not be. There was another such scene yet to come. I could scarce keep the field-glass to my eyes as the second and last body of cavalry—which was composed of light horse also—came thundering up out of the hollow.

They were not so bold as the men on the white horses, who fell, many of them at the very line of bayonets. The horses of these swerved as they came upon the ground covered with carcases, and their line was broken; but the squadron leaders rode straight to death. Once again the curling smoke spurted out from the Prussian front, and to the rear and right and left flew the survivors of the squadrons. The brown field was flecked with spots of many colours, and, trampling on the remains of that mass of strength and courage of man and horse, the Prussians, to whom supports were fast hastening up right and left and rear, pressed on towards the inner *épaulement*, and became engaged with the French infantry, who maintained for some time a steady rolling fire in reply to the volleys of the Prussians.

To me the French force seemed there very much superior in number. But they had lost courage, and what was left of it was soon dissipated by the advance of a Prussian battery, which galloped up to the right flank of their infantry, and opened a very rapid fire, to which there was no French battery to reply. The French left the *épaulement*, and made for a belt of wood, dropping fast as they retreated, but facing round and firing still. In a few moments more the plateau was swarming with the battalions of the 11th Corps, and the struggle there was over. Only for a minute, however, because, from the flanks of the wood came out a line of French infantry.

The musketry fire was renewed; but it was evident the Prussians were not to be gainsaid. Their advance was only checked that they might let their artillery play while their columns assisted it by incessant volleys. A fierce onslaught by the French, made after they had retired behind the wood, only added to their losses. The Crown Prince's army, notwithstanding the cavalry success at the outset, had by three o'clock won the key of the position of the French right with comparatively small loss.

The Bavarians of Von der Tann's corps, on whom devolved the

difficult task of carrying the village or town of Bazeilles, and Balan (a suburb of Sedan outside the fortifications), suffered enormously. They were exposed to a fire of infantry in the houses, and to the guns of the works and the musketry from the parapets. The inhabitants joined in the defence, and as soon as the Bavarians had crossed the Meuse by their pontoons and by the railway bridge, they could receive but little protection from their artillery placed on the heights.

The French made the most strenuous attempts to repulse them, in which the marines were particularly distinguished; and three divisions of Bavarians, which began to fight at four o'clock, were exposed to three distinct onslaughts from the town and from the corps under the walls. At one time it appeared as if they would be overpowered, although it seemed as if success against them would scarcely have secured the French army from its ultimate fate.

It is believed by the Bavarians that MacMahon himself was wounded very early in the day, when directing his troops in an offensive movement against Bazeilles. General Ducrot then took command of the whole army, but General de Wimpffen, producing a sealed letter, showed that he was authorized to as-sume the control of the operations of the army in case of any accident to Marshal MacMahon. The Marshal was wounded early in the morning, and, according to the reports of French officers, prisoners of the Bavarians, there was a difference of opinion between General Ducrot and General Wimpffen re-specting the plan of attack which the French adopted at one period of the day as the best means of defence.

Having beaten the Bavarians out of Balan at one time, the French made a rush in the direction of Illy, as if determined to cut their way through on the flank of the Saxon army, and pass towards Metz. But the Crown Prince of Saxony had by that time resumed the offensive, and had brought an overwhelm-ing force to block their way. They were driven back, delivering the Bavarians from the stress to which they had been exposed. Their divisions advanced once more, and Bazeilles, or as much as remained of it, was firmly occupied; but the fight about Balan lasted much later.

Here it was, according to Bavarian reports, that the Emperor, declaring that he only served as a private soldier, went with

BAZEILLES

an attacking column composed of the remnants of various regiments, to drive out the Bavarians. But the artillery on the heights above the river and the cross-fire from the heights above the road were too much for troops shaken by incessant fighting and frightful losses. Shell and shot rained fast about the Emperor, one of the former bursting close to his person and enveloping him in its smoke. The officers around entreated him to retire, and the Bavarians quickly following occupied Balan and engaged the French on the glacis of the fort I cannot say whether this was previous to the period referred to by General Wimpffen in his address to the army. He speaks therein of a supreme moment when it was necessary to make a final effort and cut their way through the masses of the enemy at any hazard. But of all that great host of 90,000 men, there were only 2,000, he says, left who answered to the appeal.

Of the remainder, there were probably 20,000 in the hands of the Prussians; but 60,000 men, deducting killed and wounded, had by this time become an utterly disorganized mass, without cohesion, 'willing to wound, and yet afraid to strike,' and crushed out of all semblance of military vitality by an overwhelming and most murderous artillery, of which the moral effect was at least as great as the physical. The bitterness of recrimination between officers and men shows that long before the battle a radical element of force was wanting. There was not only a deficiency of cordial relations in their kind between the officer and the soldier, but a worse evil still—an actual apprehension on the part of the officers of those whom they were to command, a fear to enforce the ordinary rules of discipline, lest the soldier should become unmanageable altogether.

The scene cannot be either imagined or described which occurred when the army, or that uniformed rabble, had been fairly driven in by the beaters, to be shot down at will. The French artillery had practically ceased to exist as a protecting arm. The guns on the works are ridiculously small ordnance of the date of 1815, with a few heavy pieces here and there; and Sedan, commanded completely from the south bank of the Mouse, was to all intents and purposes an open town, with the inconvenience of having a walled *enceinte* to embarrass the movements of the troops. The Emperor retired, I believe, within the place, but not, surely, for safety, but rather to escape from the

BAZEILLES

surging mass of impotent soldiery.

There was a rain of Prussian and Bavarian bombs upon the town, issued with terrified citizens who had had no time to escape. The troops outside had been fighting without food since the morning, and there were no resources within the city to meet their wants. They were in an angry and terrible mood, upbraiding their officers, mutinous; and every shell that fell increased the evil of their spirit. To one of many missiles was now reserved a great mission.

A shell fell into a warehouse or manufactory in which was stored some inflammable material. A vast volume of flame rushed for a moment into the air, and a volume of thick white smoke, which towered and spread out so as to overshadow half the city, gave rise to apprehension on one side and expectation on the other that some central magazine had gone up. But no noise ensued. Still, at the moment, the resolve was taken that Sedan and all that it contained should be placed in the power of the victor, in the belief that it was impossible to resist with any prospect but that of ruin, complete, however lingering.

Another writer describes the cruelty of the Bavarians to the inhabitants and defenders of Bazeilles; out of which they were driven several times by the gallantry of the French marines. Almost to this day the place remains a heap of ruins. The observer alluded to writes:—

Bazeilles was near the Meuse, and near Sedan: the inhabitants of the village, on hearing of the arrival of the enemy in the neighbourhood, donned their National Guards uniforms, and tried to hold in check a Bavarian corps, and a division of Prussian reserves. The French were driven back, and the Prussians entered the town; it was said that shots were fired from the windows of private houses upon the Prussian troops; be this as it may, it is certain that a scene of horror, and nameless excesses then commenced, that must for ever disgrace their perpetrators. In order to punish the inhabitants of the village for presuming to defend themselves, they set fire to the place. The population sought refuge in the cellars. All—women and children—were burnt alive! Out of 2,000 inhabitants, barely 300 survived to relate how the Bavarians drove the women and children back into the flames, and shot those who succeeded in escaping. A description of the village after the Prussians left was sickening—there was not a house standing. A fearful smell of charred flesh pervaded the air, and the calcined bones of the inhabitants lay on the thresholds of their own dwelling.

Although the Germans were now everywhere victorious, and were holding all the entrances into the town, still their batteries continued to bombard it, now so full of troops and material as to be indefensible, and set fire to it in several places; at five o'clock p.m. the firing ceased, and soon afterwards a French colonel, escorted by two *Uhlans*, one of whom carried a white flag, rode up to where the King had taken up his position, and asked for terms of surrender. After a short consultation between the King and General Moltke, the French colonel was informed that when the capitulation of so large an army and of so important a fortress were in question, an officer of higher rank should have been sent.

You are therefore to return to Sedan, and tell the Governor of the town to report himself immediately to the King of Prussia. If he does not arrive in an hour, our guns will open again; you may tell the Commandant that it is useless trying to obtain other terms than unconditional surrender.

Soon after his departure, the King sent Colonel Brousart into Sedan with his demand for the capitulation, who, on his arrival, was introduced to the Emperor, who wished to give him a letter for the King; on learning his mission, however. Napoleon referred him to General de Wimpffen, who was in command (MacMahon having been severely wounded early in the day by a piece of shell), and sent his adjutant, General Reille, with the letter to the King.

About seven o'clock Colonel Brousart returned, and informed the King of MacMahon's being wounded, and of the presence of the Emperor in Sedan: the King's escort then drew up in line, and the King, in front of his staff, received General Reille, who, dismounting, handed the Emperor's letter to His Majesty, saying, at the same time, that he had no other orders. King William having said, "But I demand, as the first condition, that the army lay down its arms," commenced reading the Imperial letter, since become famous, and very remarkable, when we consider its result. It ran as follows:—

Ne pouvant pas mourir à la tête de mon armée, je viens mettre mon épée aux pieds de votre Majesté.

Being unable to die at the head of my army, I lay my sword at

A Prussian Officer

the feet of your Majesty.

The King, after consulting with the Crown Prince of Prussia, who had previously joined him, and with Count Bismarck and Generals Moltke and von Boon, wrote as follows:—

Sire, My Brother,   Before Sedan, September 1st, 1870. Regretting the circumstances under which we meet, I accept the sword of your Majesty, and I invite you to designate one of your officers provided with full powers to treat for the capitulation of the army which has so bravely fought under your command. On my side I have named General Moltke for this purpose.

I am,

Your Majesty's good Brother,

(Signed)   Wilhelm.

The King handed the above to General Reille, who received it bareheaded, and then returned to Sedan, escorted by the two *Uhlans.*

On his departure the King gave General Moltke power to negotiate, and ordered Count Bismarck to be at hand in case of political complications, and then drove to his quarters at Vendresse, amid the cheers of his soldiers.

While giving the King, General Moltke, and the army, the credit of the success of the day. Count Bismarck is reported to have claimed some credit for effecting the unity of so many of the German races, who had that day made common cause, and fought side by side against the enemy in defence of the fatherland.

The Germans celebrated this great victory by impromptu candle illuminations and the singing of the usual patriotic airs; but their leaders, discussing the chances of the future, felt that there might yet be many a hard day's fighting before peace would be declared.

The situation of the French at the conclusion of the day, and while the bearer of the flag of truce was proceeding to the German Headquarters, the town was entirely surrounded by the Germans, whose well-served guns, carrying with murderous effect over 4,900 metres, planted on all the surrounding heights, dominated the place, and could have shelled it so that hardly a house would have been left standing; while the defeated French soldiers, crushed into the narrow streets with no longer any organization, were perfectly demoralized, and exasperated by their bloody but useless struggles, were ripe for mischief and much more dangerous to friend than foe.

The scene in the town was, I have heard from several of the inhabitants, of the most harrowing description: dead horses and men encumbered the ground; and horses, limbers, guns, caissons, and baggage-waggons all pell-mell, broke the surging mass of soldiers, who wandered about indiscriminately, drunk and cursing their leaders and officers, whom they threatened to assassinate. Under such circumstances what course remained open to the Emperor and his advisers but that which His Majesty wisely and humanely took?

General de Wimpffen had assumed the command of the French army when MacMahon was wounded, although the Marshal had given General Ducrot, in presence of the Emperor, orders to mass the troops behind Sedan and retreat on Mézières; whether he had orders from Paris to that effect or not is not yet ascertained, but General de Wimpffen took the command, some say under the plea of being the older general of the two, and considering the proposed retreat a false move, rashly commanded an advance, with what result we well know. That he was not wanting in courage is evident from the attempt he made to rally the troops: crying out that Bazaine was attacking the Prussians in rear, he rallied a few thousand soldiers, and, leaving by the Porte de Balan, attacked the church garrisoned by the Prussians, who were at last taken prisoners owing to the doors being blown in by cannon, but he and his party were soon driven back into the town.

Probably fresh from Africa, and full of the military traditions learnt there, and ignorant of the really inefficient and demoralized state of his troops, he thought that a good dash would restore victory to the French arms; but he counted without his host, and numberless killed and prisoners, and the immediate fatal consequences of his defeat, testify to his rashness and incompetence as a great leader; and if his name—as he is reported to have said it would—goes down to history linked with so humiliating a capitulation as he subsequently signed, he must remember that such a fate is not wholly undeserved; his wilfulness in arrogating to himself the command after MacMahon was wounded, and his rashness in counter-ordering the wise retreat the Marshal had directed, deprive him of the sympathy he would otherwise have been entitled to, and leave him without a word of defence.

The conduct of the Emperor during the battle, and amid such trying scenes, has won him the good report of those who were impartial witnesses of it. He was among his troops, encouraging them all the morning, heedless of the projectiles which fell around him, and visited several of the corps in the centre, including that of Lebrun at Balan, and re-entered the town in the belief that all was going on favourably. Later on he essayed to leave it, but found his exit prevented by the retreating soldiers and waggons; and a shell bursting under his horse in the Place Turenne killed the horse of a general behind him, but any emotion he may have then shown was not that of fear. A general, too, was killed in a *café* close by him (probably General Guyot de Lespars), and the waiter (still there) was struck by a piece of the same shell, but not killed. Finding he could not leave the town, Napoleon retired to the *Sub-Prefecture,* where, after ordering the capitulation and writing to the King of Prussia, he passed the night doubtless a prey to bitter thoughts, on which, however, it is no business of mine to speculate.

At five o'clock on the morning of the 2nd, Napoleon, accompanied by a few of his staff, quitted Sedan in one of his carriages, and proceeded towards Donchéry in search of Count Bismarck, who, warned by an officer of his advent, dressed and hastened out to meet him. The Count, in his undress uniform, met, cap in hand, the Emperor, who alighted; saying, on being requested to resume it, "Sire, I receive your Majesty as I would my own Royal Master."

Escorted by the Count on horseback, the Emperor drove towards Donchéry, and stopping the carriage near that town, alighted, and entered in company with the Count a weaver's house; but shortly afterwards came and sat outside, and a long conversation ensued, conducted principally in German at the wish of the Emperor, who was aware that Count Bismarck was no great French linguist.

The Emperor tried to obtain a favourable capitulation for his army, but Bismarck would not entertain the question at all, which, he said, being a purely military one, was in the hands of Generals Moltke and de Wimpffen. The Chancellor, however, proposed negotiations for peace; but the Emperor, as a prisoner, expressed his inability to enter into any, and referred him to the Executive authority at Paris, which alone was empowered to entertain any such proposals. The Emperor also submitted to Bismarck the question as to the practicability of allowing the French army to cross the Belgian frontier, there to be disarmed and interned; this question had, however, been propounded the previous evening, and negatived by General Moltke.

It is believed that the Emperor deplored the misfortune of the war, and stated that, though not desiring it himself, he had been forced by public opinion in France to declare it. The Emperor wished very much to have an interview with the King before the capitulation should have been signed, but the Chancellor demanded its signature

NAPOLEON III AND BISMARCK AFTER THE BATTLE OF SEDAN

HOUSE IN FRONT OF WHICH NAPOLEON
AND BISMARCK CONVERSED

first, as it was the King's wish to leave his officers to settle the terms with the French generals, reserving for a subsequent personal interview merely such matters as would directly affect the Emperor.

Count Bismarck then went to confer with the King, and the Emperor, escorted by a detachment of the 1st Prussian Cuirassiers, and attended by some of his staff, went to the Château Bellevue, belonging to a M. Amour, of Sedan, and prettily situated above the village of Frenois, on a wooded knoll sloping towards Sedan in the front, and behind towards the Meuse, from which it is about fifty yards distant: being surrounded by a small plantation and a pleasure ground, it possesses the advantage of seclusion, an object Napoleon much desired, as he wished to avoid the observation of his countrymen.

According to the best authorities, the capitulation was settled and signed by Generals Moltke and de Wimpffen in the same *château*. The terms proposed by General Moltke were considered very hard by De Wimpffen; but though the French troops were furious at the idea of any capitulation at all, the terms eventually accepted by their commander were quite justifiable, when the position of the French is considered. The town was commanded by numerous batteries placed on the surrounding heights, which would have *rained* a perfect tempest of shot and shell on the exposed town, whose streets were crowded with masses of disorganized troops, horses, guns, and *matériel*, had the question been unsettled at noon.

The town could have offered no resistance, and the troops still in the suburbs outside the gates must have been annihilated. De Wimpffen, while deploring his misfortune in having to sign such a document so shortly after his return from Algeria, yet seeing the impossibility of further defence, and the useless and sanguinary results that a continuance of the fighting would entail, subscribed to the capitulation, of which the following is the text:—

Frenois, September 2nd, 1870.
Between the undersigned, the Chief of the Staff of King William, commanding-in-chief the German armies, and the General Commandant of the French army, both being provided with full powers from their Majesties King William and the Emperor Napoleon, the following convention has been concluded:—

Article 1.—The French army placed under the orders of General Wimpffen, finding itself actually surrounded by superior

PARK OF GUNS, MITRALLEUSES &C. AT SEDAN TAKEN FROM THE FRENCH

forces round Sedan, are prisoners of war.

Article 2.—Seeing the brave defence of this French army, exemption is made in respect of all the generals and officers, and also of the superior *employés* having the rank of officers, who pledge their word of honour in writing not to bear arms against Germany, nor to act in any manner against its interests until the close of the present war. The officers and *employés* who accept these conditions will retain their arms and personal effects.

Article 3.—All arms as well as the materiel of the army, consisting of flags, eagles, cannon, ammunition, &c., shall be immediately delivered at Sedan to a military commission appointed by the General-in-Chief, in order to be forthwith handed over to German commissaries.

Article 4.—The town and fortified works of Sedan shall be given up in their present condition, at latest, on the evening of the 2nd of September, and be subject to the disposition of His Majesty King William.

Article 5.—Those officers who shall not have accepted the engagement set forth in Article 2, together with the disarmed troops, shall be marched out, ranged according to their regiments or corps, in military order. This proceeding will commence on the 2nd of September, and will terminate on September 3. These detachments will be marched to the districts bordering upon the Meuse, near Iges, to be handed over to German commissaries by their officers, who will then resign their commands to their sub-officers. The chief surgeons, without exception, will remain behind to attend to the wounded.

Von Moltke,
Wimpffen.

The capitulation signed, General Moltke went to the battlefield, where at noon he met the King, who at eight o'clock having received no news at Vendresse, drove, according to previous agreement, to the place of rendezvous.

Having notified his intention of paying his captive a visit, the King, accompanied by his staff and by the Crown Prince of Prussia, and escorted by cavalry, started about half-past twelve for the *château*, where he arrived a few minutes later.

The Emperor received his conqueror with grave politeness, and seemed perfectly calm; after a few moments' conversation, they retired

VIEW OF CHÂTEAU BELLEVUE,

alone into a little *boudoir* or glass wing off the centre rooms, where they remained about a quarter of an hour. On returning, the Emperor seemed much affected by the King's kindness and generosity, and indeed expressed as much with tears in his eyes to the Crown Prince, with whom he conversed for a few moments after the above interview. His face looked worn, but observant of all around; he frequently pulled his moustache, the ends of which were waxed as usual, but maintained his calm demeanour except for the few moments during which he was talking to the Crown Prince.

His chief anxiety was to avoid his troops, and to obtain permission to pass through Belgium, instead of through France, to Aix-la-Chapelle, *en route* for the palace of "Wilhelms Höhe," in Cassel, a palace where his uncle, King Jerome of Westphalia, had once lived, when it was called "Napoleon's Höhe," and which place the King had appointed for his residence during the continuance of the war. The King also gave him permission to take with him some of the officers of his household, his servants, horses, carriages, and baggage, and appointed General Bozen (Prussian) and Prince Synar, late Prussian Secretary of Embassy in Paris, to attend him as *aides-de-camp*.

Dr. Russell has given us some interesting notes of the conversation that took place between the two sovereigns, which, though at first contradicted by Count Bismarck's paper, yet as personally the Count denied the contradiction, may be considered authentic. Dr. Russell, writing to *The Times*, says:—

The King spoke first. God, he said, had given the victory to his arms in the war which had been declared against him. The Emperor replied that the war had not been sought by him. He had not desired or wished for it, but he had been obliged to declare war in obedience to the public opinion of France. The King made answer that he was aware it was not the Emperor's doing. He was quite sure of it.

'Your Majesty made war to meet public opinion, but it was your Ministers who created that public opinion which forced on the war.'

His Majesty, after a pause, remarked that the French army had fought with great bravery.

'Yes,' said the Emperor; 'but, Sire, your Majesty's troops possessed a discipline in which my army has been wanting lately.'

The King remarked that for some years the Prussian army had

been availing itself of all new ideas, and watching the experiments of other nations before '66 and subsequently.

'Your artillery. Sire, won the battle. The Prussian artillery is the finest in the world.' The King bowed, and repeated that they had been anxious to avail themselves of the experiences of other nations.

'Prince Frederick Charles decided the fate of the day,' remarked the Emperor. 'It was his army which carried our position.'

'Prince Frederick Charles! I do not understand your Majesty. It was my son's army which fought at Sedan.'

'And where then is Prince Frederick Charles?'

'He is with seven army corps before Metz.' At these words the Emperor started, and recoiled as if he had been struck; but he soon recovered his self-possession, and the conversation was continued. The King inquired if his Majesty had any conditions to make or to propose.

'None. I have no power. I am a prisoner.'

'And may I ask, then, where is the Government in France with which I can treat?'

'In Paris; the Empress and the Ministers have alone power to treat, I am powerless. I can give no orders, and make no conditions.'

The King on the same day sent the following telegram to the Queen at Berlin:—

From the King to the Queen.

Before Sedan, France,

Friday, Sept, 2—1.22 p.m.

A capitulation, whereby the whole army at Sedan are prisoners of war, has just been concluded with General Wimpffen, commanding, instead of Marshal MacMahon, who is wounded. The Emperor surrendered himself to me, as he has no command, and left everything to the Regency at Paris. His residence I shall appoint after an interview with him at a rendezvous to be fixed immediately. Under God's guidance, what a course events have taken!

And in subsequently referring to the same ever-memorable event, wrote:—

Varennes, Sept, 4—Morning.

What a solemn moment when I met Napoleon! He was bowed down, but dignified. I have assigned him Wilhelmshöhe, near Cassel (capital of Hesse Cassel), as his residence. Our meeting took place in a little castle in front of the western glacis before Sedan. From there I rode along the front of the army at Sedan. The reception of the troops you can hardly imagine. It was indescribable. At eight o'clock, when it became dark, I finished my ride, which had lasted five hours, but I did not return here till one. May God help us further.

In a letter to the Queen he also recurred to the meeting, and gave an account of the battle of Sedan in the following terms:—

Vendresse, South of Sedan, Sept 3.
You already know through my three telegrams the entire extent of the great historical event which has just happened. It is like a dream, though one has seen it unroll itself hour by hour. When I reflect that after one great and successful war, I could expect nothing more famous during my reign, and when now I see it followed by this act, forming part of the world's history, I bow myself before God, who alone has chosen me, my army, and my allies, to accomplish it, and has appointed us the instruments of His will. Only in this sense can I comprehend the work, in order with humility to praise God's guidance and grace.

Now for a picture of the battle and its consequences, in very brief form.

On the evening of August 31 and the morning of the 1st inst, the army had reached the prescribed positions round Sedan. The Bavarians formed the left wing, near Bazeilles, on the Meuse; next them were the Saxons, towards Moncelle and Daigny; the Guards were still marching towards Givonne, and the 5th and 11th Corps were towards St. Menges and Fleigneux. As the Meuse here makes a sharp bend, no corps were posted between St. Menges and Donchéry, but at the latter place were Würtemburgers, who also covered the rear against sallies from Mézières. Count Stolberg's cavalry divisions were in the plain of Donchéry as the right wing. In the front, opposite Sedan, were the rest of the Bavarians.

The battle began, in spite of a thick fog, at Bazeilles, quite early in the morning, and by degrees a very hot fight developed itself, in which house by house had to be taken, this lasting almost the whole day. Schöler's Erfurt Division (4th Corps of the Reserve) were obliged to take part. When at eight o'clock I reached the front before Sedan, the great battery was beginning its fire against the fortifications. At all points there now broke out a hot artillery fire, which lasted for hours, and during which ground was gradually gained on our side. The villages above named were taken.

Very deep ravines with woods made the advance of the infantry difficult, and favoured the defence. The villages Illy and Floing were taken, and, by degrees, the circle of fire drew closer and closer round Sedan. It was a grand sight from our position, on a commanding height behind the before-mentioned battery, to look beyond the village of Frenois over Point Torcy. The vehement resistance of the enemy commenced gradually to slacken, as we could perceive by the broken battalions, which hastily retreated from the woods and villages. Their cavalry endeavoured to attack several battalions of our 5th Corps, who, however, maintained their position excellently. The cavalry galloped through the spaces between the battalions, then turned round, and went back the same way; this being repeated three times by different regiments, so that the field was strewn with corpses and horses. All this we could see perfectly well from our standpoint. I cannot yet learn the number of this regiment.

When the retreat of the enemy at all points became a flight, and all—infantry, cavalry, and artillery—pressed into the town and its immediate vicinity, and when no indication yet presented itself of the intention of the enemy to extricate himself from this hopeless position by a capitulation, nothing remained but to bombard the town with the before-named battery. After it had, in twenty minutes, set fire to the town at several points, which, with the many burning villages over the whole battlefield, made a terrible impression, I ordered a suspension of the firing, and sent Lieutenant-Colonel von Brousart, of the General Staff, with a white flag, to propose the capitulation of the army and fortress. He was met by a Bavarian officer, who informed me that a French *parlementaire*, with a white flag, had announced himself at the gate. Lieutenant-Colonel von Brousart was admitted, and on asking for the commander-in-chief he was unexpectedly led before the Emperor, who wished immediately to hand him a letter for me.

The Emperor asked what kind of proposal he brought, and being told a summons for the surrender of the army and fortress, he replied that he must refer him on this point to General de Wimpffen, who had just assumed the command in lieu of the wounded MacMahon, and that he would now send his adjutant, General Reille, with the letter to myself. It was seven o'clock when Reille and Brousart came to me, the latter a little in advance; and it was first through him that I learnt with certainty the presence of the Emperor. You may imagine the impression which this made upon all of us, but particularly on myself. Reille sprang from his horse and gave me the letter of the Emperor, adding that he had no other commission.

Before I opened the letter I said to him, 'But I demand, as the first condition, that the army lay down its arms.' The letter begins thus:—'*N'ayant pas pu mourir à la tête de mes troupes, je dépose mon épée à voire Majesté*' (Translation: 'Not having died at the head of my army, I yield my sword to your Majesty'); leaving all the rest to me.

My answer was that I deplored the manner of our meeting and begged that a plenipotentiary might be sent, with whom we might conclude the capitulation. After I had given the letter to General Reille, I spoke a few words with him as an old acquaintance, and so this act ended. I gave Moltke powers to negotiate, and directed Bismarck to remain behind in case political questions should arise. I then rode to my carriage and drove here, greeted everywhere along the road with the loud hurrahs of the troops, who were marching up and everywhere singing the National Hymn. It was deeply touching. Candles were lighted everywhere, so that we were driven through an improvised illumination. I arrived here at eleven o'clock, and drank with those about me to the prosperity of an army which had accomplished such feats.

As on the morning of the 2nd I had received no news from Moltke respecting the negotiations for the capitulation, which were to be carried on in Donchéry, I drove to the battlefield, according to agreement, at eight o'clock, and met Moltke, who was coming to obtain my consent to the proposed capitulation, and told me, at the same time, that the Emperor had left Sedan at five o'clock in the morning, and had come to Donchéry.

As he wished to speak with me, and as there was a *château* and park in the neighbourhood, I chose this for our meeting. At ten o'clock I reached the height before Sedan. Moltke and Bismarck appeared at twelve, with the capitulation duly signed. At one o'clock I started again with Fritz, escorted by the cavalry staff. I alighted before the *château*, where the Emperor came to meet me. His visit lasted a quarter of an hour. We were both much moved at meeting again under such circumstances. What my feelings were, considering that I had seen Napoleon only three years before at the summit of his power, is more than I can describe.

After this meeting, from half-past two to half-past seven o'clock, I rode past the whole army before Sedan.

The reception given me by the troops, the meeting with the Guards, now decimated—all this I cannot describe today. I was much touched with so many proofs of love and devotion.

Now, farewell, with a heart deeply moved at the conclusion of such a letter.

Wilhelm.

The Emperor passed the night at the *château*, and on the following morning (3rd) about 9 a.m. the Imperial *cortège* started for Libramont in Belgium. The Belgian Government, in answer to the applications of both sovereigns, had previously given leave for the passage of the Emperor and his suite through Belgium; and the route chosen was by road through Bouillon to Libramont, a station on the Luxembourg and Brussels railway, thence through Liège to Verviers, where the Emperor was to sleep, and so by Cologne to Cassel.

The carriages were escorted by two troops of Black Hussars, who rode uncloaked, notwithstanding the heavy rain which was falling. The Emperor, accompanied by Achille Murat, was in a brougham, and was dressed in the undress uniform of a Lieutenant-General, with the Legion of Honour on his breast. To those who saw him pass, he looked pale, tired, and anxious, but still calm and free from nervousness. A long string of Imperial carriages followed, containing French and German officers, and then a number of mounted French officers, grooms, led horses, *fourgons*, &c. It is worthy of remark that the Imperial servants and horses were as well turned out and as splendidly appointed as in the piping times of peace at Paris.

Every courtesy and respect were shown to the Emperor throughout the route to Cassel, where he was received with military honours, and attended by Generals von Plonski and Grafmonts, Governor of the city of Cassel, and Captain von Dupenbrock Gruiter, commanding the hussars stationed at the palace. Among others of his recent favourites, he had with him Generals Felix Douay and Lebrun. In his temporary captivity I shall now leave him, and return to the events that took place at Sedan after the capitulation.

Having returned from signing the capitulation. General de Wimpffen had the following proclamation posted over the town:—

Soldiers!—Yesterday you fought against very superior forces. From daybreak until nightfall you resisted the enemy with the utmost valour, and expended almost your last cartridge. Exhausted by the struggle, you were unable to respond to the appeal made to you by your generals and your officers to attempt to gain the road to Montmédy, and to rejoin Marshal Bazaine. Two thousand men only were able to rally, in order to make a supreme effort. They were compelled to stop at the village of Balan, and to return to Sedan, where your general announced, with deep sorrow, that there existed neither provisions nor ammunition.

The defence of the place was impossible, its position rendering it incapable of offering resistance to the numerous and powerful artillery of the enemy. The army collected within the walls of the town, unable either to leave it or to defend it, and means of subsistence for the inhabitants and the troops being wanting, I have been compelled to adopt the sad resolution of treating with the enemy. Having proceeded yesterday to the Prussian headquarters, with full powers from the Emperor, I could not at first resign myself to accept the clauses which were imposed. It was only this morning, when threatened by a bombardment to which we had no means of replying, that I determined to make further efforts, and I have obtained conditions which relieve you as far as possible from the humiliating formalities which the usages of war usually exact under such circumstances.

Nothing now remains for us, officers and soldiers, but to accept with resignation the consequences of necessities against which an army could not struggle—want of provisions and deficiency of ammunition. I have at least the consolation of having avoided a useless massacre, and of preserving to the country soldiers who are capable at some future time of rendering good and brilliant service.

De Wimpffen,
General Commanding-in-Chief.

The scene in the town on the terms of the capitulation becoming known beggars description, and I have been assured by eye-witnesses and by the inhabitants, that the disorganization that prevailed was so dangerous, and there was such a scarcity of provisions, that the civilians were glad to receive their conquerors with civility. The men vowed they had been betrayed, and threatened their officers with assassination, and indeed General de Failly narrowly escaped their vengeance. Some were boastful, others seemed inclined still to fight, whilst a very large proportion, seeking to drown their shame in liquor, staggered about intoxicated, dangerous alike to friend and foe. Discipline was conspicuous only by its absence. Not one regiment could muster its scattered units, who wandered about a prey to conflicting passions, seeking on whom to vent their curses and chagrin.

Many of them, indeed, were wounded, but found no means available for the dressing of their wounds. Guns, waggons, and caissons blocked the extremely narrow streets; and one of the most piteous sights was that presented by the horses, who in many cases tied to gun and waggon wheels, and abandoned by their riders, and furious with hunger, squealed and kicked in their endeavours to get free, and many of them succeeding in their endeavour, dashed wildly about in their paroxysms of fear and hunger. Dead horses were cut up and eaten by the soldiers; human corpses lay here and there; abandoned arms and equipment of all kinds littered the streets; the rain poured down in torrents, and the streets seemed a perfect pandemonium, and presented an ever-changing scene of horrors to the unwilling observer. With reference to the destruction of arms I should add that quantities of arms of all kinds, equipment, and even *mitrailleuses*, were thrown into the Meuse to prevent their falling into the enemy's hands, and the eagles were burnt or broken up. Indeed, fishing arms out of the Meuse afforded amusement to the German garrison for many a day afterwards.

19,000 French troops succeeded in escaping into Belgium, where they were disarmed and interned; and a similar fate befell a large number of German wounded. The wounded of both sides were sent to Namur.

On the 3rd Sedan was delivered up to the Germans, and the French prisoners, accompanied by many of their officers, who refused to give their parole not to fight against the enemy during the rest of the campaign, were marched out to a great camp formed on the peninsula made by the bend of the Meuse, according to the terms of the convention. Luckily no collisions occurred, owing to the exertions of the French officers and to the judicious management of the Germans, who avoided as much as possible any direct contact with their prisoners.

The prisoners were afterwards sent to Germany under escort at the rate of about 10,000 a day.

About 95,000 prisoners fell into the conquerors' hands, besides an enormous number of guns and horses; in fact persons in the vicinity bought up horses for five and ten francs apiece. The number of cannon and *mitrailleuses* taken was very large, and they covered acres of ground when parked, and many of them were used by the Germans in their subsequent sieges of Verdun and Mézières.

I have chosen the following as one of the most complete accounts of the after-scenes on the field of battle. The correspondent of the *Daily News* writes as follows:—

The evacuation of the town has gone on in earnest today. Already there is a great camp on the peninsula within the bend of the Meuse. The prisoners taken in the battle have gone away in strong detachments, guarded by German troops; and those who were upon the rainy, muddy road to the rear last night, as was the present writer, saw columns of Frenchmen tramping briskly along, with the German escort marching by their side in the worst of humours at being so employed, and with blankets muffled over the men's heads to keep off the rain. Well might the villagers stare at so novel a sight—their own countrymen blocking the way, but blocking it as prisoners—their own uniform dragged to prison, as if it were a capital crime to be a Frenchman.

The poor folks seemed chiefly anxious to avoid further loss, and chiefly suspicious of soldiers of any kind. But it was clear that amid all their terror and all their fear of downright starvation, they had a warm corner in their hearts for the lads of their own language and nation. I have seen many women today cooking for the prisoners and trying to push through the crowd to bring them small dainties. In the church at Donchéry there were hundreds of French soldiers collected this morning. Cavalry and infantry. *Zouaves* and *Cuirassiers*, huddled together in marvellous fashion. The smart, dashing men whom we have seen when we travelled through France were reduced to a condition of semi-shabbiness and blank despondency which was something new to see. They were wont to be the gayest fellows in the world, and here were rolled up, tumbled over, and generally 'done for,' by men whom they had been rash enough to despise.

I rode over the greater part of the battlefield yesterday morning—the morning after the fight. It was a shocking thing to see so many dead men and wounded men, and dead and wounded horses, crowded together in some places. It was a sight to cause reflections, as the old Frenchman said who lived in the village where the fighting had been hottest. "*Ah! mon Dieu, monsieur, c'est là la guerre.*" He took a sombre view of *la guerre*, for the scene was horrible. With two friends who were anxious to study the positions of the armies contending on September 1st, I went round through Donchéry and past the great bend of the Meuse, came towards the French lines as the 11th Prussian Corps had come, and pushing southward between the outposts of the hostile armies, traversed the railway bridge at Bazeilles, to return to headquarters.

The first sign of active and immediate war was the block of prisoners at Donchéry. There they were, of all arms of the service, the dark-faced *Turco* and the young boyish conscript, collected in a mass, ready to be marched away. The plain beyond Donchéry was covered with slightly-wounded men wandering to the rear. French and German, friend and foe, it mattered not; they went amicably along, the common suffering making them friends. No one seemed to dream of further violence and farther fighting. The battle was over, and they were glad to creep together to the rear, with little civilities exchanged in the way of pipe-lights and sips of brandy, and with no more hostile feeling than two patients already in an hospital.

We passed hundreds of them as we went round the bend of the stream and came upon the first signs of the conflict of the day before. There was a dead horse, a *cuirass*, a heap of broken weapons. In this cottage were several wounded Frenchmen, taking some soup with a wounded Prussian, who seemed almost too much hurt to eat. Behind the garden wall was a dead *cuirassier*, his hands clutching the grass in the agony of death, his face stern and determined. No one noticed him any more than if he were a dead horse. In quiet England whole districts will turn out to see a murdered family, and here on a battlefield the same murdered family would be trampled into the mud without being noticed. This meadow on the hill-side is full of mangled horses and dead *cuirassiers*.

It was here that they made a frantic attempt to break through, and were mowed down by the Prussian fusillade. You must have been on several battlefields to understand the signs of what has taken place by the look of the spot next morning. This group of dead horses, with a helmet or two and a dozen *cuirasses*, with a broken trumpet and three dead *cuirassiers*, means serious work. The dark stains on the ground are where the wounded have lain and been removed. The little heap of swords under that hedge is where some dismounted troopers were forced to surrender. Then we come to Prussian helmets crushed and trampled. Some are marked by shell or bullet, and have blood upon them. They tell of loss to the regiment to which they belonged.

Others have no particular trace of violence, and may either be signs of wounded men, or of men who have simply thrown their helmets away in the heat of action, and put on their forage caps to march more lightly. These dark stains, surrounded by knapsack and rifle, by greatcoat and cooking-tin, are where men have lain who have been badly wounded, or even killed, but whose friends have made them as comfortable as could be under the difficulties of the time. One has a little shelter of twigs and branches put to keep off the sun; another has had a blanket propped on two rifles, and his knapsack for a pillow. But he has died in the night, and is left with his cloak over his face until the burying party shall come round.

See yonder drums and knapsacks, stains of blood, and dead men lying on their faces. It is where a blow has been struck at some infantry regiment The men have fallen under a musketry fire, and the line of dead shows where the ground was held. Come a few steps further to the rear. You perceive a few more dead men, shot whilst in flight, and a number of bright, well-cleaned rifles scattered on the turf. This is where the regiment broke and fled, where some perished with their backs to the foe and others threw down their arms. We might gather the minutest details of the loss on either side if only human strength and energy sufficed to traverse this immense tract in a single morning. When another day has passed, and the dead are buried and the arms collected, it is difficult to judge of the fight by seeing the ground; whilst on the third or fourth day, the dead horses become so much decayed that, until they are removed, it is well-nigh impossible to move about where they have fallen.

All honour to the helpers of the wounded—to the regular and volunteer hospital assistants. Their red-cross badge must be a joy to many a sufferer; and though some who wear the badge seem disposed to "loaf" about rather than to be helpful and active, yet the greater part do their duty well. The better sort of volunteers in the work—the Sisters of Charity and surgeons who have donned the badge—are full of zeal. Some of the best families of Germany are represented among these helpers of the wounded; there are several foreigners, too, engaged in the common cause of humanity.

Thanks to all that is done, the wounded are so soon removed to villages, or placed under some sort of shelter, that even next morning there are but a few of them to be seen on the ground. They are being brought to the nearest ambulance waggon on stretchers, with many cries and groans. Heaven help them! or are lodged in a cottage near the field, or are carefully bandaged up and laid on straw, and sent jolting painfully away in country carts to a more remote hospital.

We found the hillside north-west of Sedan covered with dead men and horses. The village in the hollow between the hostile lines was not much knocked about, and there were few shell-marks on the road leading up to the summit. But once arrived at the point where the Prussian fire had begun to tell, we found traces of its terrible effect Here lay a dead horse in the middle of the road, with saddle and bridle, just as it had fallen. Here was a Frenchman shot through the head, behind a small clump of earth, where he had taken shelter in skirmishing. Then there were several more horses and men lying upon the road; and at length a slight breastwork to either side, carried along the ridge of the hill, and full of French soldiers who had died in its defence. The ground began to be ploughed up with the shell-fire from the opposite rising ground, where the Prussian artillery so long remained. Near the two trees and the cottage prominent on the summit, were traces of the sharp fighting which I had observed the previous day.

A *mitrailleuse* battery, of four pieces, was surrounded with dead bodies; horses and men were lying on all sides—I cannot quite say in heaps, but very thickly scattered. At one place there were horses as thick as they could lie. But this was a little farther down the slope to the southward, where I had seen that gallant cavalry charge. The Chasseurs-à-cheval and the Chasseurs d'Afrique had dashed along the hillside, half-hidden in the dust which they raised, and had been destroyed by a steady fusillade. Here lay the famous light horsemen, with their bright uniforms dabbled in blood, and their fiery little steeds crushed and mangled by Prussian shells.

Most of the men and horses now on the ground were dead, but some few wounded men yet lingered in agony, with white rings tied to sticks that were planted beside them as a means of calling the surgeon's attention when he should have time to revisit them. The badly wounded horses, more fortunate for once in being brutes, had been killed to put them out of pain, and only a stray horse slightly wounded stood dismally here and there, wondering, perhaps, what it could all mean.

Behind the scene of the light cavalry charge is a ravine that separates this shoulder of the rising ground from that immediately above Sedan. In the ravine there had been great slaughter at the end of the fight, when the French were crowded together from different points. Up behind the woods on the farthest summit of the rising ground was all the *débris* of a rout. It had been clear, even from a distance, that the beaten army struggled hard. Yet, nevertheless, they had been beaten, and here were arms thrown down, waggons abandoned, caps and coats, swords and rifles of every branch of the service, lying scattered on the ground.

Some considerable body of troops, cut off from Sedan by the advance of the Prussians, had tried to break through to the town, and had been dispersed or captured. The whole of the northward and north-eastward slopes, at what we may call from this side the country, at the back of the town, showed traces of this crowding together and of the heavy cross-fire of German artillery, which had begun so soon as the circle of the attack became narrowed to a sufficient degree. Nearly 100,000 men, as now appears, were hampered and shut in by less than 200,000 of their enemies. No amount of devotion could extricate the French army when once it had become the centre of a converging fire.

The ghastly wounds inflicted on most of the French dead, whom I saw upon the hill, showed that they had fallen under an artillery fire, and the ground was in many places so ploughed up that a blanket could scarcely have been laid on it without covering some spot where a shell had exploded. The thick woods at the back of the town were full of wreck and rubbish—abandoned waggons, with the dead horses at the side, to show why they had been so left; stores of biscuit, harness, and soldiers' knapsacks were still very plentiful as one approached the village of Bazeilles, southward of Sedan, where the Bavarians had fought.

The village was on fire, and the streets presented shocking sights to scare away the inhabitants again for a couple of days more, should they now return. The half- burnt bodies of Frenchmen and Bavarians were being brought out from among ruins, and laid by the roadside. Men yet living, but terribly wounded and scorched, were moved on litters to beyond the stifling smoke of the conflagration. There was reason to fear that many poor lads had been literally roasted when the fire came upon them, and their wounds forbade all hope of escape. This village was, perhaps, the gloomiest part of all the acres of pain and death spread around Sedan. The interior of the town itself is said to be very much injured, but that I have not yet had time to visit

On the 3rd September the advanced guards of the German army started for Paris. The 3rd Army proceeded by Montmirail, Coulommiers, and Briecomte-Robert, while the combined army marched by the valley of the Marne. In order to carry out this arrangement the two armies had to cross each other's route, and this their wonderful organization enabled them to do at Rheims. My military readers will appreciate the magnitude and danger of such an operation, and its successful issue speaks volumes for the excellence of the staff. The subsequent acts of these armies are now well known, and they pass out of further notice in these pages, leaving us astonished at the magnitude of their successes.

That Bazaine by some means or another was aware of the date on which MacMahon should have been in his vicinity is evident from the fact that on the 31st August he attacked the 1st Army Corps of Prussians,, the division of General Kummer, and the 4th Landwehr division on the east side of Metz in great force; but though the French fought through the night till the 1st September, they were beaten back at all points by the Germans, who by means of a telegraphic cordon they had established were enabled rapidly to concentrate their troops to repel them.

This sortie of Bazaine's convinces me that though MacMahon's attempt to relieve Metz was a very rash and dangerous strategical movement, yet that had he marched more rapidly and warily it is quite possible his object might have been achieved, and fresh lustre been added to the arms of France. The material he had at hand, however, was to a certain extent very inferior; and much of the bad inarching of the French may, I think, be ascribed to the ridiculous system of overloading their soldiers, who are required to carry the enormous weight of 75 lbs., made up as follows, *viz.*:—Chassepot rifle, 7½ lbs.; bayonet and scabbard, 3 lbs.; ammunition, 93 rounds, 10 lbs. (distributed in pouches and knapsack); 1 pair of shoes; canvas havresack, greatoat, blanket, pair of trowsers, comb, brushes, housewife, 2 pair socks, 3 shirts, 4 lbs. rations, water bottle, canvas of *tente d'abri*, and some of the sticks for it, a camp kettle to every five men.

Besides the above many of them carry entrenching tools. The Prussians on the other hand have an equipment very similar in weight to our own, and carry 72 rounds of ammunition. They have their knapsacks carried for them on carts whenever expeditious marching is required. This was the case before Sedan, and doubtless to this wise provision much of their success may be attributed. To enable them to do this the Germans have the Prussian Intendantur system, based on the principle of dividing and subdividing the responsibility into different sections, and applied even to regiments; in opposition to the French centralization system.

Each German *corps d'armée* has its provision column, divided again into five columns (under proper officers), and all liable to be subdivided into smaller bodies if required; each division or subdivision has a responsible head, and any errors or shortcomings can at once be brought home to the right person. The infantry battalion, about 1,030 strong on active service, has its ammunition waggon, a cart for the regimental books and pay chest, a hospital cart, an officers' baggage *fourgon*, and 18 horses, A cavalry regiment, about 700 strong, has four squadron waggons, one officers' baggage waggon, one field forge, and a hospital cart, for the draught of which 16 horses are allowed.

Each artillery regiment has nine ammunition columns, consisting of 49 waggons and 344 horses, subdivided into two divisions to supply ammunition to the guns, as well as for the small arms of the cavalry and infantry.

Besides these the artillery have further large reserves of ammunition to feed the afore-mentioned columns.

With so excellent an organization it cannot be wondered at that there was never a want of ammunition in the field; and this contrasts most favourably with the French *Intendance*, which frequently failed to supply the troops in action with ammunition, besides suffering from the constant breakdown of its provision trains. The Emperor's advisers preferred the system of centralization, basing it on the supposition that it would be too expensive to maintain separate *matériel* for every regiment.

The French *Intendance* monopolizes all the supply and transport branches of the service, and nothing can be done without reference to the central authority. The delays this caused to the French in the late war may be easily imagined, and the inconvenience and difficulty of expansion of the system condemned it at once when placed in *juxta*-position with that of Germany. Rapid movements are essential to success in modem warfare, but no commander can advance unless assured of supplies of provisions and ammunition for his troops; and the dilatory movements of MacMahon are in a great measure attributable to his anxiety on that pointy as not all the gallantry of his best soldiers could compensate for a want of supplies and an ill-managed *Intendance*.

But I must not dilate on what is at once so interesting and so important, lest I should stumble lamely through a subject that has already been so ably treated by prominent writers of the day; but before summing up the principal causes of the failure of the French arms, I intend to touch very lightly on the rifles and cannon of the contending armies. Scientific and professional men have already so well discussed their respective merits that it would be idle on my part to pretend to express any opinion concerning them; but as all of my readers may not have cared to purchase the high-priced volumes in which many of those opinions have appeared, I devote a few lines to give the result of a contest, the issue of which exercised so great an influence on the more important battles of the campaign.

As the needle-gun of the Prussians was the first breech-loading rifle that by its successful use attracted the attention of Europe, I shall give it the precedence.

It was first patented in England in 1831 by a Mr. Moser, and on an improved principle was first issued to the Prussian troops in 1848; and though it has undergone certain modifications in its construction, the weapon of the present day varies but little from that of '48. For those who desire a detailed account of its mechanism, I think I cannot do better than refer my readers to Captain Hozier's work on the war, published in parts, in which I believe a very interesting description of its working, as well as that of the *chassepot*, will be produced.

The *chassepot* was the pet weapon of the late Empire, and was on its trial during the recent war. It was invented especially to compete with the needle-gun, and its superiority to the latter has certainly been proved in the severe test it has undergone. The *chassepot* has an initial velocity of 1,328 feet per second; the needle-gun of 990 feet per second. At 300 paces it scatters nearly double what the needle-gun does—this is a disadvantage. It can be fired 10½ times per minute, while the needle-gun can only be discharged 7½ times.

Its cartridges are smaller, and consequently more of them can be carried—a great advantage in the eyes of a French soldier, who fires in a great measure at random, and presents a great contrast to the phlegmatic and cautious Teuton. It carries effectively 1,800 yards, while the needle-gun can be depended upon only up to 600 yards. The advantage of so long an effective range must be patent to the most casual observer, but the French soldier nullified this great advantage by his random firing. Had it been in the hands of the Germans it would have been murderous in its effect; and they themselves frequently acknowledged to me its superiority.

The *mitrailleuse*, another introduction of the Imperial *régime*, did not quite answer the expectations previously formed of it. Without an engraving of it it is difficult to explain its construction. It is in reality a series of rifled barrels, which by an ingenious mechanism discharge about twenty-five balls at each turn of the handle the soldier makes; the director is able to discharge one or all almost simultaneously. As the cartridges are ready fixed in the feed-cases, which are placed in the *mitrailleuse*, the process of reloading is very quick, and great rapidity of fire can be attained. It carries about 2,000 yards, but is not considered a great success, on account of its too concentrated delivery;

where it strikes all must go down, but the area over which it spreads is very small, and this defect diminishes its importance as an effective weapon.

The French guns were chiefly muzzle-loading bronze four and six pounders, carrying 15 lb. and 9 lb. shells respectively; while the Prussians used breech-loading guns of similar weight and calibre. The trajectory of the French gun, however, was very highly curved, owing to the shape of the missile it projected and the length of bore, and its initial velocity being small the ball starts at a lower rate than that from the Prussian gun, and opposing a larger area to the resistance of the air it loses its velocity quicker.

The Prussian breech-loader was open to this objection, however, which I believe condemns it amongst artillerymen in England, that after a few rounds there was often great difficulty in opening the breech.

The Prussian concussion shells were much more effective than the French shells exploded by time fuzes, because the former striking the hard ground exploded most effectively, while the time fuzes generally burst the French shells in the air, and it was much more difficult to calculate the range.

The same remark applies to the artillery fire as to that of the chassepot; the French fired so rapidly that they wasted most of their ammunition, while the Germans, quite cool and acting on very strict scientific principles, burst nearly every shell most effectively, and the concentration of the fire from all points on the unfortunate remnant of MacMahon's army at Sedan, was a most successful and well-directed tactical feature in the day's manoeuvres of so enterprising and well-served an artillery.

But before passing on to finish my task, one most important feature in the German armies that in a great measure conduced to their superiority over the French; one cause of success that while adding to their mobility blended the units of the army into a sentient machine; and for the absence of which no superiority of weapon or organization could or would have compensated, must not be overlooked.

Many of my readers will have anticipated what I am about to refer to, and will endorse my views as to the excellence of the German drill.

The Germans used the company as their unit for manoeuvring; the French, the battalion.

In 1847 the Prussians adopted the system of manoeuvring by

companies; their battalions were composed of four companies, each about 250 strong, with a mounted captain. Each battalion can at any moment be broken up into four small columns, which are formed by the breaking up of each of the four companies into three subdivisions, each about 80 strong.

The captain thus commands a handy little battalion, which he moves independently, unless otherwise ordered by the officer commanding.

It is needless to say that when this change was first proposed it met with much opposition from the majors and field officers, but the practical advantages of it when tested in war became too apparent to allow their prejudices to stand in the way of its adoption, and the present system is nearly identical with that propounded in 1847.

In the recent war the company column formation of the Prussians has stood the severest practical tests, and come victorious out of the contest; wherever the fighting was close and desperate; whenever rapid movements were desirable, then and there it was resorted to, and invariably with success. Covered by skirmishers, these small and handy columns ever held the ground they gained, and were not too unwieldy to negotiate the difficult positions they so frequently had to attack; besides which their numerical weakness enabled them to find cover where a battalion would have stood but to have been decimated. The system is at once so handy and convenient for the operation of the breech-loader, and yet so loose, that none but highly-disciplined troops, possessing an unshaken confidence in their officers, could be trusted to work by it; but applied to the German armies it met with unmeasured success; and even when a temporary check was received, or a retreat inevitable, no want of cohesion ever presented itself, or permitted a retreat to become a rout.

Whether such a system could be successfully applied to the French army is open to much doubt; but it could not experience a greater breakdown than that which befell the battalion unit system of the French, They still stuck to their old traditions, but trained their men to a looser method than before, and in also employing masses of skirmishers rendered them very mobile. But the free use of skirmishers necessitates an amount of discipline, self-reliance, and confidence in the officers that the French latterly wanted, and that which proved an element of success in the German army became a source of danger and failure in the French.

The cavalry drill, too, of the Prussians was excellent, but its chief merit lay not in the combined movements of the mass, but in the instructions which guided its units in making reconnaissances, in keeping up the communications of the armies, in gaining information of all kinds, and in so covering the flanks and front of the advancing Teutonic hordes that the ill-informed and badly-served French generals never knew whether their presence was due to the exigencies of foraging, or whether it implied the propinquity of the main army. The ubiquitous *Uhlan*, a name misappropriately applied to all the German light cavalry, is a European term herited from the late war; and the whole cavalry force by its gallantry and dash have achieved a well-deserved reputation.

With regard to its influence on MacMahon's march towards Metz much might be said, but I restrict myself to the following remarks:— It gave the information that enabled the Bavarians to surprise the French at Beaumont, and the 3rd and 4th Armies to combine on the 30th of August, and captured numbers of prisoners, guns, and stores from the retreating and routed columns of the enemy. It covered the advance and swinging round of the 3rd Army, and at the battle of Sedan materially assisted in effecting the northern junction of the two German armies.

I have alluded to the excellence of the German artillery in a previous paragraph, and I only desire to ascribe here much of its success to the admirable Prussian tactical direction by which it was worked; the gist of all of which is that direct fire by masses of artillery is of little avail, and to be avoided, but that while batteries should be attached in great numbers to an army they should have a common object to concentrate their fire on, and at the same time should do so from such different positions as will enable them mutually to bring a heavy cross and enfilade fire, if possible, to bear on the point of attack. And further, rather in opposition to our own traditional instructions, that artillery should act independently of infantry support.

How ably the German artillery fulfilled its mission and acted up to these instructions at Sedan, and how completely its batteries enfiladed the fortifications of that fortress, and assisted the attack on Bazeilles and Balan, we have already seen; but I do not entirely go with those who give it the only place of honour in the success at Sedan, or attribute the French defeat there to its influence alone. I rather incline to ascribe all that took place there to a variety of causes, of which it, however, forms an important one. And this appropriately leads me to the conclusion that from this battle, as indeed from all those that preceded it, I am justified in deducing the following causes of failure :—

1st. The enormous difference in point of numbers between the contending armies; the Germans having in this battle more than double the strength of their adversaries.

2nd. The incapacity of the French *Intendance* to furnish supplies of ammunition, provisions, and stores.

3rd, The high state of organization of the German armies, descending to such minor details as identification tickets and grave-digging corps.

4th. The wastefulness of ammunition of the French when using their *chassepots*.

5th. The admirable concentration of the German artillery fire on certain points from different positions, and their numbers, weight of guns, range, and precision of fire. The first Napoleon used his artillery in much the same way; and the Germans attacked Bazeilles under cover of its fire, and crossed the river Meuse, getting close to the French centre, under cover of the fog, as Napoleon I. did at Austerlitz.

6th. The disparity between the training, education, and position of the French and German officers.

7th. The want of strategical genius to make up for the German superiority in numbers.

8th. The strategical knowledge displayed by the Germans, by means of which masses were brought to bear on smaller bodies, and armies and corps separated and beaten in detail; and armies converged towards each other and met at a given place on a given day with mathematical accuracy.

9th. The unity of command in the German armies, by means of which through the King, as Commander-in-Chief, implicit obedience was yielded to General Moltke's strategical directions, and the complete chain of military command brought to bear on the execution of them.

10th. And lastly, the inferior discipline and want of cohesion in the French army, as compared with the discipline, steadiness, and wonderful intelligence displayed by all arms of the German service; and especially by the artillery in their knowing when to advance unprotected by infantry, and what advantageous positions to take up; and by the cavalry, in their scouring the country for intelligence, deceiving the French as to the whereabouts of the main body, and enabling their commanders to surprise the French, ever heedless of such precautions, as at Beaumont, where De Failly's corps was surprised and routed: all of which shows the absolute necessity of teaching an army in time of peace as far as possible the system that it must follow in time of war.

And before proceeding farther, I wish to lay before my readers the meaning of the word discipline, as laid down by Colonel Hamley, as I shall use it in two or three places farther on:—

Discipline is a union of very different qualities, each of which is an important element in war. It means cohesion of the units and suppleness of the mass; it means increased firmness and increased flexibility; it means the most efficient combination of many and various parts for a common end.

Most people limit the causes of the misfortunes of the late war, and the inefficient state in which the declaration of war found the French army, to the luxuries of the Empire and the system of centralization prevailing in every department; but in my humble opinion, if we look below the surface, we shall find much to account for the failure of the French arms in the political state of the army at the outbreak of the war.

Without doubt the nation, of which being conscript the army was to a certain extent the reflex, had for the last forty years been amassing enormous wealth, and had latterly harried to make money to be spent in the pleasures of the capital at a railroad pace. The Emperor, understanding his people, had fostered this commercial ambition, and sought to secure the future of his dynasty by enriching their hearths and homes, and by associating his name with every great enterprise in art, literature, or commerce, as his uncle's already was with the national military glory.

The court was most luxurious, and among an imitative *bourgeoisie* everything became subservient to money.

The army did not escape the prevailing mania, and its luxuries and excesses were winked at to keep it in good humour till, demoralized by the material comforts of civilization, it became enervated by a second Capua. The pleasures of a luxurious life made fighting unpleasant to the mass on the first reverses, and devoid of the patriots' feelings, the scorn of death no longer was their heritage.

The aristocracy of the army, however, and indeed the mass of the officers, did not spare their best blood to stem the torrent of invasion; and fighting, as the educated officers of every country have ever fought, gave their lives for their country, preferring death to dishonour, and added to the roll of those brave men whose loss France is now lamenting.

Amongst the lower ranks, too, there were gallant exceptions, and at Sedan, as on other battlefields, here and there groups of dead soldiers were found, who back to back had met their fate, weapon in hand, and face to the foe.

I pass over the unfortunate breakdown of the *Intendance*, and of the want of organization at the commencement of the campaign, and I come to the political cancer that had eaten into the heart of the French army; the pernicious doctrine of equality; eighty years before it had infected the nation, and then while luxuries and absinthe ruined their physique, this insidious moral poison instilled itself into the veins of the army. Discipline, as already defined, and sub- ordination are essential to the success of an army, but how can they exist alongside equality. The soldier thought himself equal to his officer, and yielded but an unwilling obedience. When promoted, having never learnt to obey, he was seldom fitted to command.

No wonder success was wanting. To ensure it to an army requires obedience, discipline, an absence of self, a thirst for knowledge, a disregard of danger, and the cheerful endurance of hardships, added to a perfect organization in the civil departments. Politics must be entirely excluded from it, and unfortunately these elements of discord were but too present in the French army.

In what I have written I trust I have given no cause of offence. A more gallant army never faced an enemy, and its heroism and valiant deeds do not suffer by comparison with the doings and traditions of a past century; but I have only tried to touch on some of the causes of its temporary failure to beat back the invader; causes which doubtless by this time it has itself eradicated.

The German army on the other hand has had a different watchword, which has successfully carried it through the fiery ordeal it has just undergone—obedience to constituted authority; there is the clue to its success; the main-spring that, having set in motion the whole, has maintained its units, performing with assured regularity their allotted task. No insidious poison has been there, working to defeat the object of the guiding hand; the master mind, planning the most marvellous and wise combinations, the result of sound practical study, has had but to turn the key and set the machine in motion, confident of the success that must follow the movements of a body so constituted.

The Prussian army, of which the other German armies are exact copies, is the representative of a well-organized monarchy.

The King, its head, though a perfect autocrat, while following the principles laid down and maintained during two centuries by his wise and brave ancestors, has led the cause of progress, and adopted such changes and reforms as are calculated to strengthen his own power, while improving the condition of his people. Simple in his habits, and frugal to a degree, he has imparted a healthy tone to society; and the army, composed of all classes of the people, conscript in the widest sense of the word, has not failed to imitate so good and so high an example. The officers as a rule belong to the aristocratic portion of the community, and while exacting implicit obedience from those under their command yield implicit obedience to their superiors, and are an element of strength to the Crown and the army.

The soldier is sufficiently educated by a paternal Government to appreciate the fact that unity and obedience, which constitute discipline, are essential to success in military matters; and he therefore sinks his political identity for the two or three years during which he is called upon to serve, and becomes a living machine, thinking only on such occasions as his superiors require him to; and at the conclusion of his service he carries back to his family the habits of order and discipline he has acquired in the army, and his children, and consequently the nation, cannot but profit hereafter by his influence.

The officers, instead of spending their time at the *cafés*, and wasting their energies under the influence of absinthe, direct their attention to the studies of war, theoretical or practical, as they may have opportunity, and gain the confidence of their men and a knowledge of their temperaments and habits by a judicious intermixture, and by showing their fitness for command.

Under such a system, where no link of the chain is wanting to bind together king and peasant, where all have had for years but one common object in view, who can wonder at the success achieved? One national ambition has influenced the whole, and while raising the Prussian monarch into a German Emperor has disintegrated the neighbouring empire, and humiliated the people who made them drain the cup of degradation to the dregs after Jena. Under such a constitution, and with such a people, whose motto is *"For God and for the Fatherland,"* what great things may yet be done! What great things have already been achieved!

One great cause of the German success that must not be overlooked is the excellence of its staff, which has from its honoured chief to its lowest grade evinced such wonderful intelligence, and materially contributed to the national success. Another is the perfection of the German equipment, and the organization of their admirable control departments of various branches; and I think I may fairly ask the nation, Have we these?

My remarks have already exceeded the limits I had intended, but I cannot conclude without a few words on the gallantry and patriotism of Marshal MacMahon, whose name will ever be identified with the Battle of Sedan.

With reference to his strategy before Sedan we must remember that he was terribly hampered by the instructions he received from the Government at Paris, and the tardiness of his movements in the march from Rheims towards Metz may be in some measure attributed to the inferiority of a large portion of his troops, and of the inability of the *Intendance* to forward his supplies. His personal gallantry on all occasions, his great tactical skill, and his patience and endurance under defeat must ever stand forth as bright spots in his military career; and I trust in holding him up in these pages to the British soldier as one whose gallant deeds are most worthy of emulation, I shall not be overstepping the limits of military etiquette. Whatever his faults and the mistakes he committed, no dishonourable act has ever been imputed to him; and while the position he now holds in France shows the estimation he is held in by the nation, his name will go down to posterity as of one *sans peur et sans reproche*.

If I have said ought to offend, my professional zeal must stand charged with it, as I have written these few pages with feelings of the highest admiration for both armies. Where two contend one must fail; but it is not always the victor who comes best out of the conflict.

And thinking of the consequences of a battle and of war in general I cannot omit to give my humble testimony to the self-denial and unsparing efforts of the agents of the International and other Red Cross societies to alleviate the miseries of the sick and needy, exposing themselves willingly, as they did, both male and female, to dangers of which many of us in our quiet English homes can form no idea. In the hospitals, on the field of battle, and on the line of route from place to place, they encountered difficulties and ran risks which must have been seen to be appreciated; and though occasionally some injudicious members of their craft clashed with the authorities, and were very properly excluded from the service, still they did as a body a vast amount of good; and many a convalescent soldier has returned to his home and people to speak with grateful recollection of the kind hand and sympathizing foreigner, who bound up his wounds and lightened his hours of weary pain.

Military writers will without doubt deduce much that will prove valuable and instructive to us from the incidents of this great war, of which the battle of Sedan forms so interesting a feature; and leaving to them a task so difficult, and yet so necessary, I turn to Colonel Hamley's *Operations of War*, written some time since, and there find a passage which conveys in much clearer and more suitable terms than any in which I could hope to express it, the lesson I desire to convey from the result of this great war to the military student and the public at large; and that is:—

Not that numbers and wealth must prevail, nor that great generals are heaven-born; it is on the contrary that the conditions of success are attainable and capable of demonstration; that the preparation of study and thought is essential to skill in war; and that being thus prepared, a leader, in order to achieve the most notable successes, need not be gifted with inspiration, but only with the more appreciable, though still rare combination of sound sense, clear sight, and resolution.

"Strategy and Tactics Defined"

Having lately heard much discussion as to the correct definitions of the military terms, "Strategy" and "Tactics," and having seen them recently misapplied, I venture to lay before my readers the definitions of those terms as given by several well-known military writers, in the hope that those who do not endorse them, more especially referring to those in a position to speak with some weight and authority, may be induced to express their views on the subject in the public journals, and thereby profit the public in general, and the military student in particular.

To save trouble to those who may not have time to search for themselves, or who do not know where to lay their hands on books likely to contain definitions of these terms, I append extracts in full from the works of Jomini, Humbert, Ambert, Hamley, and Macdougall, all celebrated writers on military subjects, whose opinions are generally received as authorities by the curriculum of military history.

In the *Etudes Tactiques* of General Baron Ambert we find the following passages:—

> *Si l'officier désire connaître la tactique du champ de bataille, c'est-à-dire la combinaison des armes entre elles, il doit avoir recours à l'étude particulière et consulter les ouvrages qui traitent de la guerre. Or, ces ouvrages le transportent, sans transition, du terrain de manoeuvre de la garnison, dans le domaine de la stratégie, que Napoléon Ier nomme la 'grande tactique.'*
>
> *Ce domaine est celui des généraux en chef. L'esprit de l'officier particulier s'y trouble, et son regard se perd dans l'immensité de savantes combinaisons.'*

The Baron evidently intends the above definition of "*la grande tactique*" to represent what we know as "Strategy."

While he defines "Tactics" as follows:—

Il existe cependant un domaine intermédiaire qui serait celui de la 'petite tactique,' tactique du champ de bataille, et qui consiste à connaître l'emploi d'une arme associée et opposée aux autres armes,
C'est, dans la science de la guerre, la partie utile aux généraux, colonels et officiers supérieurs. C'est le côté pratique du métier de chef de colonne et de commandant de ligne.'

Baron Jomini in his *Précis de l'Art de la Guerre*,[1] in explaining the five heads into which he divides the art of war, writes:—

La 2ᵉ est la stratégie, ou l'art de bien diriger les masses sur le théâtre de la guerre, soit pour l'invasion d'un pays, soit pour la défense du sien.
La 3ᵉ est la grande tactique des batailles et des combats.
La 6ᵉ est la tactique de detail,"

(2. Strategy, or the art of properly directing masses upon the theatre of war, either for defence or for invasion. 3. Grand Tactics. 6. Minor Tactics.[1])

Humbert, *chef d'escadron*, gives a more elaborate definition of these terms in a work published by him in 1866, and I subjoin selections from it:—

Stratégie.—La stratégie peut être définie la science des conceptions et des directions; elle consiste à faire la guerre sur la carte, et à déterminer le plan de campagne: c'est la science nécessaire au général en chef.
De la grande tactique,—La tactique en campagne sert à appliquer les manoeuvres aux opérations de la guerre; c'est sur le caractère des nations qu'elle doit être basée, aussi diffère-t-elle ordinairement suivant les peuples.

And here he appends in a footnote an extract from the writings of Jacquinot de Presle, which we might almost imagine he had quoted in anticipation of the late war, and which contains advice his countrymen unfortunately neglected following:—

Footnote,—*Ainsi, chez un peuple vif, susceptible de passions violentes, la rapidité des mouvements et l'impétuosité dans l'attaque sont nécessaires; tandis que pour une nation calme et tranquille le feu sera l'un des premiers éléments de sa force.*

He then goes on to say:—

---

1. *The Art of War* by Antoine Henri Jomini, (in English), also published by Leonaur.

La stratégié combine et dirige de grands plans, la grande tactique les exécute, et par conséquent lui est subordonnée; celle-ci s'apprend, celle-là est pour ainsi dire innée.

A défaut de règles absolues à poser, les souvenirs de l'histoire ont servi à établir un certain nombre de principes généraux."

Footnote.—*Ces principes, qui ont de tout temps existé, n'ont été dévoilés que récemment, à la suite des opérations de Bonaparte en Italie et du Prince Charles en Allemagne. Alexandre, Annibal, et César les avaient devinés; Gustavo Adolphe, le Prince Eugène, Turenne, et Frédéric en avaient fait de belles applications.*

Pour pouvoir appliquer judicieusement l'art de la grande tactique, il faut connaître les divers ordres de bataille en usage, les manoeuvres et les marches, les positions militaires, enfin le mécanisme des batailles.

Observons en outre que toute méthode de guerre doit se modifier suivant la configuration du terrain, et suivant le moral on les mouvements habituels des adversaires. Des manoeuvres in variables ne pouvaient amener à la longue que des revers.

In Burn's *Dictionary* I find the following definitions of Strategy and Tactics:—

Strategy.—Science of military command, and of all the operations of war.

Tactics,—Science of military movements made in presence of an enemy, and within reach of his artillery; the tactics of a soldier are the correct performance of military movements; those of the officer, to know how to direct their execution; and those of a general, to combine them in such a manner as to ensure success.

Colonel Hamley, now a writer on military subjects of European fame, gives a long but comprehensive explanation of these two military terms. He commences by summing them up briefly, and giving the key to their meaning as follows:—

The theatre of war is the province of Strategy.—The field of battle is the province of Tactics.

Continuing, he says:—

It is the object of Strategy so to direct the movements of an army, that when decisive collisions occur it shall encounter the enemy with increased relative advantage.

If two armies advance towards each other till they meet, both equally covering their own communications, and equally ready to concentrate for action, it is evident that Strategy has no share in the result; for all that has been done is to bring them face to face, and leave it to force or tactical skill to decide the issue. Bat when the movements of one of two armies have been so directed as to increase the chances in its favour, by forcing the enemy either to engage at a disadvantage, or to abandon territory under penalty of worse disaster, there is proof of a power which differs from the mere ability to fight.

The purely military advantages to be attained by strategical operations are of two kinds: 1st. The probabilities of victory; 2nd. The consequences of victory.

The triumph of Strategy is complete when the commander of one side succeeds, by the combinations of the campaign, in bringing his adversary's army into a position where the chances of victory are greatly against it, and where defeat will entail disasters beyond the loss of the battle.

Strategical movements have the following objects:

1st. To menace or assail the enemy's communications with his base;

2nd. To destroy the coherence and connected action of his army, by breaking the communications which connect the parts;

3rd. To effect superior concentrations on particular points.

Colonel Macdougall, in his *Theory of War* treats them in the following manner:—

The arbitrary distinction which has been made by military writers is that Strategy relates to the movements of an army on the theatre of war, when not in actual presence or eyesight of an enemy, however great or small the distance which separates them; while Tactics relates exclusively to the movements of an army when in the actual presence or eyesight of an enemy. The following definition applies equally to both:—
Strategy and Tactics are the art of placing in a certain position at a certain time (meaning the right position at the right time) a body of troops in fighting order superior to that body which your enemy can then oppose to you.

In the *Penny Cyclopaedia* we find Strategy defined as follows:—

Strategy (from the Greek **στρατηγία,** which may be translated 'Generalship') is, properly, the science of combining and employing the means which the different branches of the art of war afford for the purpose of forming projects of operations and of directing great military movements: it was formerly distinguished from the art of making dispositions, and of manoeuvring, when in the presence of the enemy: but military writers now, in general, comprehend all these subjects under the denominations of grand and elementary tactics.

Strategy consists chiefly in making choice of convenient bases (fortified places or strong positions), in order to place there in security the military establishments of an army; such as the barracks, hospitals, and magazines of ammunition and provisions, previously to commencing offensive operations, or in contemplation of the army being compelled to act on the defensive. In the former case, it may be necessary to decide on undertaking the siege of some fortress on a frontier, for the purpose of holding the neighbouring district in subjection, and commanding the roads by which it may be thought convenient to penetrate into the enemy's country, or by which the provisions and warlike stores may be brought up to the immediate seat of war.

In the latter case, choice is to be made of positions strong by nature, or which may be made so by art, in order that the army may be enabled to dispute the ground gradually, to harass the enemy by frequent skirmishes, or to prevent him from receiving supplies by intercepting his convoys on the roads.

Tactics are defined in the following terms:—

Tactics **(τακτικός)** properly signifies the art of forming the troops of an army in order of battle, and of making changes in the dispositions of the army of either, according as circumstances may require.

I think I have quoted from sufficient authorities to enable my readers to arrive at a definite conclusion as to the correct meaning of these two terms, and also of the manner in which they should be applied in referring to the incidents of a campaign; and I shall conclude by giving as the result of my researches the definitions, kindly sent to me by Colonel Chesney, R.E., and inserted with his permission, and which it seems to me, while embodying the views of the others, condense the terms in which they are expressed, and in terse and concise language convey their meaning to the student, and leave but little opening for further controversy:—

> An armed contest is in general, as Clausewitz shows, composed of a number of distinct and complete acts, which are in fact the actions, and which form units of themselves. From this subdivision of a campaign or war there arise two separate functions: the one being '*the arrangement and management of the troops in action;*' the other, '*the employment of actions for the general purpose of the war.*' The first constitutes 'Tactics;' the second, 'Strategy.'
> Or, as the same authority elsewhere more briefly summarizes it. Tactics teach '*the use of forces in action;*' Strategy, '*the use of actions towards the object of the war.*' A definition based, in my opinion, on principles much sounder than those in ordinary military text-books.

Battlefield of Sedan

C. W. Robinson

Contents

Introduction

So much interest attaches itself to the scenes of the late war Between France and Germany, that now that peace has removed the difficulties which heretofore beset the traveller in the attempt to reach Sedan or Verdun, Gravelotte, Metz, Spicheren or Saarbrück, there will doubtless be many tourists who will avail themselves of the return of quiet times and summer weather, to drive along the broad French *chaussées* connecting these historical spots, and spend a night or two in the little *auberges* of the neighbourhood.

To such, an account of a fortnight's visit to these scenes at a time when the traces of the day at Sedan were fresh upon the ground, when Metz and Verdun still held out,—when Prussian Uhlans, as they patrolled the roads, were unhorsed by the *Franctireur's* shot—and the ambulance flag drooped at every few yards from the village windows, may be of interest, and, perhaps, also of use in enabling them to realize more clearly what has gone on around them.

If anyone who reads these pages forms from them a more just idea than he had previously held of either French or Germans, or finds them of service in helping him to picture the spots and incidents to which they refer, the writer will feel glad that he has published them.

As he made his journey in company with another officer upon the Staff, whose account of the war *From Sedan to Saarbrück* is now familiar to the English public, he must apologize for two things—first, for the mention of many matters which may perhaps only be of interest to military men, and, secondly, for the necessary similarity in parts between what is related by him, and by his fellow-traveller.

CHAPTER 1

From England to Sedan

In the month of September, 1870, the interest of the war between France and Germany was not, as subsequently, centred around Paris; but was nearly equally distributed between the march of the Prussian King towards the French capital and the opposing hosts of Prince Frederick Charles and Marshal Bazaine around Metz. The journals of the day were filled with the accounts of the great Battle of Sedan, which had just been fought. The burning of Bazeilles and other incidents of that battle—the Waterloo of the third French Empire—were in everybody's mouth, and the telegrams each morning announced the progress of the sieges or blockades of Strasbourg, Toul, Montmédy, Mézieres, Verdun, or some other fortified place of more or less importance in the north of France.

It was under these circumstances that we (the writer and a friend), anxious to see something of the stirring military scenes that were going on abroad, and preparatory to leaving by the express train, *en route via* Dover, Ostend and Brussels for Sedan, entered one of the London Clubs. The first thing that met the eye upon entrance was one of those pencilled telegrams upon thin tissue paper, so familiar since the war broke out. This announced that:

> Cholera and typhus fever were raging in the vicinity of Sedan, and that the air was tainted by the battlefield for twelve miles around.

As we read this, thoughts of abandoning the expedition flashed, we confess, through our minds. We were neither of us about to travel to the theatre of war from mere curiosity, but were both (I believe) animated with the hope that we should gain by it in professional knowledge. Still even the thirst for this may be carried too far, and had we felt an unshaken faith in the truth of telegrams in general, we should probably not have taken our tickets, as we did, for Ostend that day.

Fortunately we had no such faith, and thought it worthwhile to verify the report nearer to the locality itself, and a very quick passage across the Channel, and a two hours' railway journey brought us safely to Brussels, where we soon satisfied ourselves that the telegram had no shadow of foundation.

It was necessary to spend a day at Brussels, part of which we passed very pleasantly with the officers of a Belgian Battery of Horse Artillery, the remainder being well filled up in the necessary preparations for our journey to the frontier, A few of the inhabitants of Brussels had gone a day or two after the battle to the field of Sedan (which lies just beyond the Belgian boundary line), and these having found every crust of bread eaten up, and every house and inn full, and every horse and cart employed, had been obliged to travel about hungry and shelterless on foot. Their hardships had so impressed themselves upon others in Brussels, and through them upon us, that we determined to leave all baggage behind at our hotel, and make the purchase of a haversack, which we half filled with provisions, in the portable form of tongues, dried beef, and chocolate, and very glad we afterwards were that we had done so.

A passport, too, (and of recent date), was a *sine quâ non*, and had to be obtained at the British Embassy. We wonder, by the way, if the majority of those who, like ourselves, have travelled long enough to remember old passport days, always filled up the blank space upon the passport left for "Signature of the bearer." An *attaché* at the Embassy having kindly told us that for want of this precaution two English M.P.'s were suspected by the French at Montmédy of false passports, and were within an ace of being shot as spies, we had the curiosity to refer subsequently to an old passport we had brought with us, and to our horror found that this space had been left blank by us since 1857, and that we had thus for thirteen years been travelling about with a suspicious document. Why this omission, however,—stupid though it may be—should be considered very suspicious, it is difficult to understand, for an erasure would almost certainly be detected, and also for an impostor, who could write, to till in his own name at leisure would be simple enough.

During the evening we met with an adventure, which we think is, for the sake of human nature, worth relating.

We could not find the way to a certain shop, and so asked a respect-able-looking man to direct us to it. He immediately fastened upon us with that eagerness and excess of attention which, if prolonged, invariably becomes a bore, and when, as was the case in this instance, it is accompanied by a long tale of reverse and poverty, generally excites a suspicion of the pureness of its object.

He told us that he and his wife had kept a school for English girls in Paris, but having lost all his pupils in consequence of the war, and not being a Frenchman, had left the city and come to Brussels in search of employment, that (producing a printed card with Hugo Kiechbach on it) he hoped we could recommend him to someone as a teacher of languages, for that he was in real distress, and knew nobody, and was that day actually in want of food. When we found the shop he did not leave us, but insisted upon accompanying us back again (two miles or so) to show the way. We did not want his company, and, in short, it soon became a question with us as to whether we must give this impostor (for so from his garrulity we set him down) something to get rid of him, or submit to his eternal society.

Self-interest, and a sense that he had been useful to us—(it was certainly not a feeling of charity)—gained the day, and assuring him that we could on no account bring him further, and raising our hats politely, we explained that we thought, under the peculiar circumstances of his case, he could not be annoyed by our desiring to be of some pecuniary service to him. To this offer he replied, that he was very grateful to us, but that he could not receive money assistance, and only hoped that we could obtain him pupils. Nothing could persuade him not to see us home; and so see us home he did, refusing to the last all our offers of money, and an invitation to enter the hotel. Now this man certainly gained nothing from us, and we came to the conclusion that by regarding him, though naturally enough, from a suspicious and English point of view, we had done an injustice to human nature in general in his person. Possibly some other suspected foreign impostors have been equally ill-judged, and we should be glad to hear that this one has since got on well in Brussels.

The following morning, with one small haversack filled to its full capacity with provisions and a change of clothes, and with our passports duly signed, and *viséd* by the French authorities, (the Prussians declined to *visé*, saying that any permission to travel must be given by the military authorities on the spot), we set off, without uniform, for the Luxembourg Railway Station, and with a ticket in our pockets for Libramont—the point at which it was most convenient to leave the line of rail in order to reach Sedan.

Before taking a final farewell of Brussels, we will mention that we bought there two of Reymann's maps (special *karte*)—one of the country around Sedan, the other of that around Metz. These maps (there are sheets of them for the greater part of Germany and France) were much used by the Prussian officers, in 1866, and are specially recommended by Von Môltke himself. For a small and portable map they are very clear and good, giving all details except the more recently constructed railroads, which can be put in at once from any ordinary railway guide. We found them to be invaluable to us.

It was 6.30 a. m. when we left Brussels, and travelling *via* Namûr, we arrived about 11.20 at Libramont, a small unimportant station.

Here we found a diligence, a clumsy, lofty, lumbering affair drawn by three horses, and waiting to take people to Bouillon and Sedan. Not having expected such a luxury, we allowed ourselves to he cut out by a rush of Belgians, who had dashed from the train to secure places, and had accordingly to be content with the best open space we could squeeze into among the trunks and baggage on the roof. As we journeyed on towards Bouillon we had a very uncomfortable time of it, our attention, when not attracted by some object of interest on or near the road, being generally devoted to the (question of whether, without danger of falling off, we might change the position of the especial limb which was suffering from cramp. But there *were* many objects of a deep interest to withdraw our thoughts from ourselves. The whole of the scenery between Libramont and Bouillon, consisting of long, undulating hills, cultivated and covered with forests, which lose themselves in rich grassy valleys, is strikingly picturesque, and as we drove along the poplar-lined *chausée* we soon came upon the first signs of the near presence of war.

Ambulances of all kinds containing wounded soldiers—some but slightly hurt, smoking tranquilly, others looking as if worn out completely by lengthened pain, passed us at frequent intervals. Waggons captured from the French with "*Intendance Militaire*" printed upon them, but now driven by German soldiers, and conveying stores and provisions, covered us with their dust. Sisters of charity raised their small boxes, with "*pour les blessés*" on them, to us as we passed, and received, I remarked, from my fellow-travellers, principally Belgians, liberal contributions, given in a manner, and often accompanied by a word denoting their heartfelt respect for those who asked their alms.

The red cross waving from the various vehicles on the road, or painted conspicuously on their sides, showed how vast was the amount of misery which demanded this stream of carriages for its alleviation; and, as if this were not enough, the picture of the dark side of war was filled in by the figure of a lady, veiled and in deep mourning, who was being driven from the direction of the field, where she had almost certainly lost some one very dear to her.

After a three hours' drive through a scene like this, we reached Bouillon, and might, had we so chosen it, have gone on at once to Sedan, but even at the loss of a day, we preferred to show our papers to the Belgian commandant and to consult him as to our future movements. As a matter of wise precaution, we had determined beforehand upon always doing this at any town of importance directly after entering it; and to the fact of our having strictly adhered to this rule, to our always seeking rather than avoiding sentries, and to our having a fair knowledge of the language, we attribute it, that we were permitted to go to places and see things which we otherwise certainly could not have visited or seen, and kept clear of those unpleasantnesses of "arrests," and so on, which travellers have so often met with in this war. These may frequently, we believe, be traced either to passports improperly filled in or signed, or to loitering about, as if anxious to avoid observation.

Bouillon is the last town of importance towards the French frontier, and so we went to see Colonel Charmet, the commandant, he was very kind, and gave us a paper requesting every one "to give us assistance;" but, by a curious absence of mind, inserted one of our names, which is an essentially English one, as "Mr. Von Alvensleben." What a German soldier or a French *Franc-tireur* would have thought about an Englishman with such a name we did not know, and we were so anxious about it that we paid a second visit to the commandant to have the error rectified.

On this occasion we asked him if he would advise our endeavouring to see something of the theatre of active hostilities, and thought a visit to it practicable. This he gave a peremptory "No" to; and on one of his *aid-de-camps*, (who having less responsibility and more youth, sympathized evidently with our wish),— suggesting that he thought it very feasible,—turned upon him with a "How can you, Sir, give such advice as that? How would you as a soldier receive a man in civilian's clothes in your lines? Would you show him very much; and mightn't you perhaps shoot him?"

"No," said the *aid-de-camp*, "I certainly wouldn't shoot him, provided he had a passport."

"Humph," replied the colonel; "well, at all events, you'd send him back again on foot, the way he came."

This was evidently in the colonel's opinion, who was a cavalry officer, nearly as had a punishment as the shooting, and the *aide-de-camp* was temporarily silent, but only to follow us afterwards downstairs and tell us not to be frightened by the "No" the chief had given us .

It was rather amusing to us while at Bouillon to hear the Belgian villagers speak of the number of prisoners they had made. The disarmed French were looked upon (of course, I mean by the common people) as their own, and not German prisoners. *"Nous avons fait beaucoup de prisonniers"* was their common expression, delivered in tones of great self-satisfaction.

As far as we could discover, no *strong* bias towards either French or Germans existed among the villagers. A great impression seemed to have been made upon them by the way in which the French wounded were "neglected," (a natural consequence of defeat,) compared with the German wounded. Numbers of the former were spread over Belgium, tended with the greatest kindness by the people—while the latter had almost all been sent (*i. e.*, those who could bear to be moved) to Germany in waggons.

The German successes, and the feeling that the French were more of a burthen to them, had, we suspect, however insensibly, tended to cool the sympathy which was originally, we believe, warmer towards the French. This, however, is only our impression; and, even if it were just, it would merely be attributing to the Belgians a very ordinary weakness of human nature.

We were fortunate in obtaining a room and beds at the *Hotel de la Poste*, the inn where Napoleon stopped on his way as a prisoner towards Cassell.

Deschamps, a Belgian *gendarme*, on duty at intervals before the inn, told us how he had seen him drive away from the door with his staff, and with "tears upon his cheek," and on our doubting the *literal* truth of this, he asserted it again and again with vehemence, as a plain fact which he would not admit of having questioned.

Deschamps was of great use to us. He showed us the way everywhere, and told us how we should best see the field of Sedan, which he had visited.

One disinterested piece of advice he gave greatly amused us. This was it:—"Only one thing," (with his finger to the side of his nose,)

114

"don't attempt to bring away arms. The Prussians search everyone on the frontier, and have said that anyone found with arms shall be shot." "If" (after a pause) "you do want anything of that sort, come quietly to me, for I've a *chassepot* and a sword-bayonet concealed that I don't mind selling you."

The Poste inn was comfortable enough as far as rooms went, but the sickeningly nauseous odour from the cattle stables which pervaded it was worse than anything we ever remember to have met with, either in Bohemia or Spain, which is saying a very great deal. One wonders how pestilence is not always rife in places of this kind.

An hour was spent, before it grew dark, in visiting the fine old stronghold of Godfrey de Bouillon, whose ancient towers watch over the opposite side of the Meuse, and within the walls of which we saw some French prisoners walking about—the first we had met with.

After our return, and while we were preparing for bed, an appeal was made to us to come down and explain what some Prussian officers who had just arrived wanted below. The inn people either did not, or would not, understand their wishes, which were to obtain a conveyance, and go on through the night having important business) towards Sedan, and when they did at last comprehend them, persisted that it was "impossible," and as a result the Prussians were obliged to sleep on a shake-down of straw until the morning, when they managed to hire a horse and trap. How they must have longed for the power to annihilate the few miles of neutral territory which intervened between them and the French boundary towards Sedan, where their slightest nod was law.

The next morning we were off at 6.30 a. m. (again on the roof of the diligence) towards Sedan, and after a drive along steep hill-sides clothed with wood, which we should have enjoyed far more upon a less swaying and lofty conveyance, we crossed the Belgian frontier and descended at La Chapelle.

Those who visit the field of Sedan will find it more convenient to descend at La Chapelle than to proceed on to Sedan at once. Between this village and Sedan itself lies much of especial interest, and it is the better plan to see this well upon the road to Sedan, and next day to visit those portions of the field lying in other directions.

As one enters the village of La Chapelle a little house (one of the first on the right hand side) is seen with a sign, on which are printed the words "Lambert, *Aubergiste*." To this house we had been recommended at Bouillon for a guide, in the person of Lambert *fils*, and as we found him all that had been told us, we recommend him to others.

His lameness, youth and speech reminded us both of the description of Erkman Chatrian's *Conscrit* of 1813, and, like the latter, he could walk well in spite of being "*boiteux.*"

CHAPTER 2

Outline of Plan and Movements of the Battle of Sedan

Before describing what we saw on the battlefield, we may mention that both the plan of operations and events of the Battle of Sedan are, for several reasons—but principally on account of the extent of the field, the long turning movements of the Germans, and the numbers engaged—not very easily understood at first sight. The accounts of correspondents and letters from the seat of war, excellent though they may be, can seldom give a full narrative of what goes on beyond their own immediate sphere of observation, and we ourselves found that it was a somewhat difficult matter to obtain, when upon the ground, a satisfactory notion of what had gone on. The ubiquitous Crown Princes of Prussia and Saxony seemed to be continually marching in a circle and fighting at about five different points of the compass at the same time, and the French facing now to their front, and now to their rear, in as puzzling a manner.

Considering that our difficulty may be felt by others, and remembering what a boon a short but connected description of the main design and features of the battle would have been to us at the time, we have thought it worthwhile to give such a description here (collected from the Prussian official account, a French pamphlet by an officer of the Emperor's staff, and other good sources), and have added a map which will both illustrate this and our wanderings over the field,

A perusal of the remaining pages of this chapter will make, we hope, the whole of the circumstances of the struggle clearer to visitors to Sedan, but those who do not care to understand the object of the particular movements of the armies had better skip them, as they must be necessarily somewhat dry.

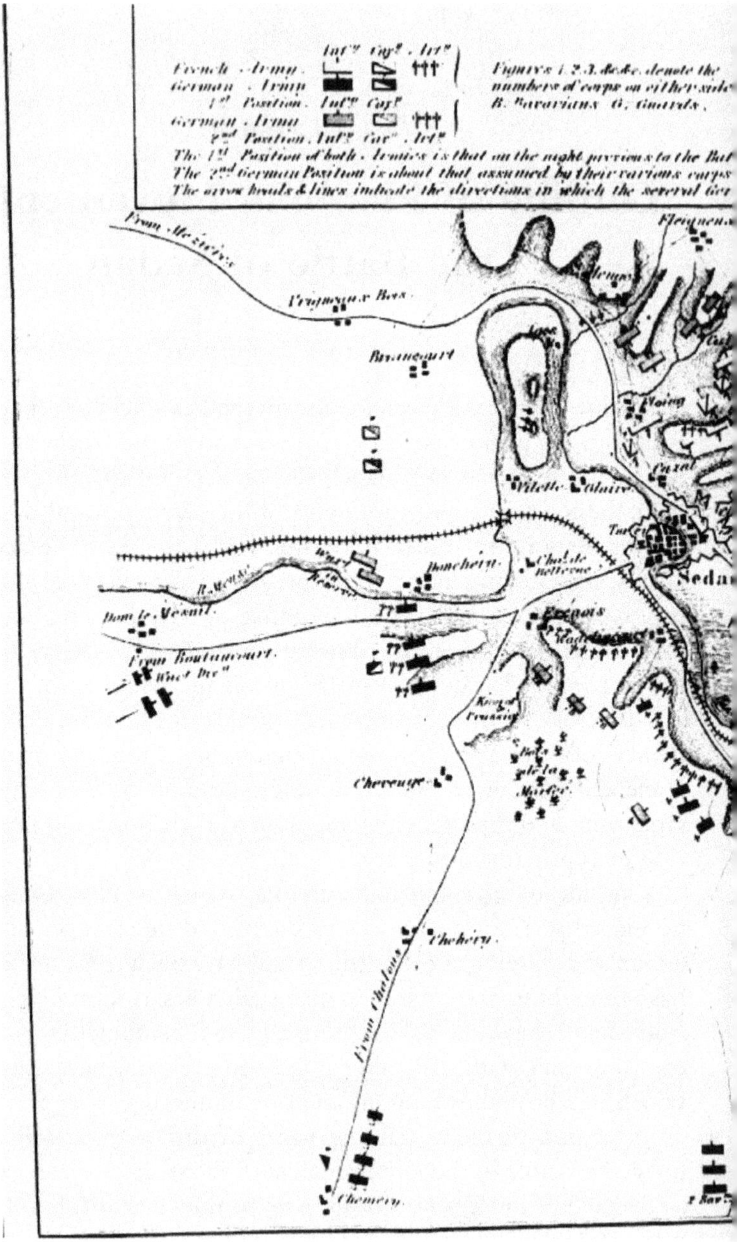

French Army.
German Army.
1st Position.
German Army
2nd Position. Inf.y Cav.y Art.y

Figures 1.2.3. &c &c denote the numbers of corps on either side. B. Bavarians G. Guards.

The 1st Position of both Armies is that on the night previous to the Bat...
The 2nd German Position is about that assumed by their various corps...
The arrow heads & lines indicate the directions in which the several Ger...

From Mezieres
Fleigneux
Frogneux Bois
Baraucourt
Illy
Floing
Cazal
Vilette Calaire
Torcy
Sedan
R. Meuse
Donchein
Chat de Bellevue
Dom le Mesnil
From Boutancourt
Fresnois
Magdeburg
King of Prussia
Bois de la Marfee
Chevenge
Chehery
From Chalons
Chemery
2 Bav.

Plan of the
BATTLE FIELD OF SEDAN.
1st Sept.r 1870.

Scale of English Miles

On the evening of the 30th and morning of the 31st of August, the French army, under Marshal MacMahon, having retreated in some disorder before the Germans and fallen back behind the Meuse, took up the following defensive position, with the determination to make a stand against the enemy:—

The 7th Corps (General Douay) was posted upon the high ground between Floing, near the road to Mézières, and Calvaire d'Illy.

The 1st Corps (General Ducrot) along the ridge between Givonne and La Petite Moncelle, occupying the villages of Givonne, Hayliès, and Daigny, and pushed forward also to the high ground east of them.

The 12th Corps (General Lebrun) from La Petite Moncelle to Bazeilles, occupying the villages of La Petite Moncelle, La Moncelle, and Bazeilles and the eastern height.

The 5th Corps (General de Wimpffen) partly in Sedan and partly on high ground to the east of it.

This position was in many respects strong—*i.e.,* the whole of it was along tolerably commanding ground; the two wings rested upon the Meuse, an unfordable river, which, by means of dams, had been made to overflow and inundate the low ground between Sedan and Bazeilles; Sedan was a fortified town, and the various villages covering the line were capable of a good defence.

Its weak points were that from the heights upon the other side of the Meuse, the line from Bazeilles to Givonne could be enfiladed by artillery; the lines of retreat were very bad, for the army could only fall back towards France by defiling round by the Mézières road, or by crossing the bridges of the Meuse, which river, it can be seen, takes a very awkward bend to the north of Sedan, so that troops retiring across it between Iges and Sedan must traverse it twice. For a defeated army to cross many narrow bridges under fire is a dangerous operation, generally ending in confusion, rout, and disorder.

Sedan, though fortified, was commanded by heights on all sides, and if these were taken it became untenable.

There is no doubt, we imagine, that the French army was at this time in a very despondent state, and by no means in good discipline. The officers probably had no great control over their men, and things were allowed to take; their chance. It is, at all events, evident that no sufficient precautions were taken to watch the German movements; the course of the Meuse was not properly guarded, and the enemy's attempt to turn the position not, as far as one can judge, ever considered as a possibility.

The German army extended round the French that evening in a large semi-circle. On the German right the patrols of the 12th Corps were close to Villars Cernay and Francheval, its advanced guards were at Pouru aux Bois, Pouru St. Remy and Douzy, and the bulk of the corps at Mairy (a mile south of Douzy).

The Corps of Guards was behind towards Carignan.

The above troops were under the command of the Crown Prince of Saxony.

The Third German Army, under the Crown Prince of Prussia, continued the semi-circle thus (all being on the left bank of the Meuse):—

1st Bavarian Corps at Remily.

2nd Bavarian Corps at Rancourt, about three miles southwest of this.

5th Corps at Chémery, west of Rancourt.

11th Corps near Douchéry.

Wurtemburg Division at Boutancourt, four miles or so west of Douchéry.

The 4th Corps was near Sedan, and properly belonged to the army of the Crown Prince of Saxony. The 6th was coming round by Attigny and Semuh, some eighteen miles to the southwest of Douchéry, to try and interpose between the enemy and France,

It was thought by the German commanders that the French might endeavour to make off in the night westward towards Mézières, and in order to intercept them, if they did so, and also in the event of their standing to surround their position, orders were issued for the 11th Corps and the Wurtemburg Division to cross the Meuse in the night, which they did by throwing bridges below Douchéry and at Dom le Mesnil, some two miles or so to the west of it.

At daylight the 11th Corps, followed by the 5th from Chémery, and by some cavalry, were to march northwards towards Briancourt, the Wurtemburgers remaining near Douchéry as a reserve. At the same time a general attack was to be made by the rest of the army, as follows:—

The 1st Bavarian Corps was to cross the Meuse by throwing bridges near Remily, and also by passing the railway bridge south-west of Bazeilles—which by some extraordinary oversight on the part of the French was not blown up—and attack Bazeilles and Balan. Part of the 4th Corps and all the Corps Artillery were to assist in this.

The 2nd Bavarian Corps was to move up towards Wadelincourt,

south of Sedan and Frénois.

The 12th Corps (leaving a reserve at Mairy) and the Corps of Guards were to move against the French line between Givonne and La Moncelle—the former on the left, connecting itself with the 1st Bavarian Corps. As the Guards were the longest distance off, they could not come into action until sometime after the 12th Corps.

From the direction of the Belgian frontier, it can be seen, that if the advance of the Crown Prince with the 11th and 5th Corps was sufficiently quick to intercept the French, they had then no way of escaping from their position, except by breaking through the German army, or retreating into the neutral territory of Belgium, where they would be obliged to lay down their arms, or incur the hostility of England.

The Germans also, it will have been noticed, had reserves at Douchéry and Mairy, near the two main lines along which the French would desire to break out—*i.e.*, towards Mézières and Carignan.

The force of the German army was double that of the French. It is said that the strength of the former was about 230,000 men and about 600 guns; of the latter 110,000 men and 440 guns.

At daylight the whole of the German army was in motion, and at Bazeilles a very determined opposition was made to the 1st Bavarian Corps. Part of the 2nd came to its assistance, but it was not for several hours that the French were driven out of Bazeilles, and also of Balan, and thrown back towards Sedan. Fighting went on here till the afternoon, and an attempt was made by the French to break through towards Carignan, but in vain.

The 12th Corps had a very hard struggle near Daigny and La Moncelle, but in the end took both these villages, driving the French from their position. La Moncelle fell about 9.30; Daigny about 12 o'clock.

The Corps of Guards arrived (coming through Villars Cernay) in time for part of it to support the fighting towards Daigny and Hayliés. The whole French line from Givonne to La Moncelle being at last forced, 100 guns were got upon the captured ground to play on the enemy, and the Guards (supported by the 12th Corps following them) passed on through Givonne towards Illy to try and encircle the enemy.

In the meantime the 11th Corps, on the extreme German left, followed by the 5th, had reached Briancourt about 7.30 a. m. without meeting the French, and then received the order to move towards St. Menges. It here came into collision with the French, who had thrown out troops to that point, and who retreated after a sharp resistance to the main position on the tongue of land above Floing and the high ground extending from this village towards Illy.

The Crown Prince now prepared to attack this high ground. The 11th Corps took up a position at St. Menges. The 5th moved round by Fleigneux. Artillery from favourable ground near these villages played for a long time upon the French, and at length, about one p. m., the Prussian infantry advanced across the low intervening ground and stormed the hills, driving the enemy back from the direction of Floing and Illy, through the woods of La Garonne upon Sedan.

The fighting between Illy and Floing was very severe, and several cavalry charges were made along the Spar above Floing, but were immediately repulsed by the breech-loading fire of the Prussian companies.

The ground near Illy having been thus carried, the 5th Corps at 3 o'clock joined with the Guards coming through Givonne the cavalry moved round to block up the road to Bouillon, and with the exception of a few hundred French, who had previously escaped by the opening between Illy and Givonne into Belgium, the whole of the enemy's army was then surrounded by a well-connected circle of Germans, which drawing closer and closer drove it down in confusion into the fortress of Sedan, where it lay at the mercy of a commanding artillery.

After half an hour's shelling from the guns posted near Wadelincourt and Fresnois, the French Emperor sent out and demanded terms.

CHAPTER 3

The Field of Sedan

As we passed through the village of La Chapelle we saw many convalescent French wounded standing dejectedly near the doors of the
houses where they were billeted. One poor fellow was sitting doubled
up by the road side with his arm in a sling and his face buried between
his knees; another had an empty sleeve, and a third, who had his head
swathed round with bandages, made signs to us to show that his chin
(a fearful wound, after which one was surprised at the man's living)
had been completely torn away.

Through the open door of the church, which (like almost all the
churches in the neighbourhood) had been turned into a hospital, the
surgeons and nurses of the Ambulance Hollandaise could be seen
moving about, dressing and attending to their patients, and on the
church walls the splintered stone showed where one or two of the
German shells had struck.

Still no damage of great consequence was done to La Chapelle by
the German artillery.

Such sights of desperately wounded men fill one with pity, and
though nothing tends more readily to your intentions being suspected
than to be seen in conversation with prisoners or wounded men, we
exchanged a few words with them in the streets, and offering a cigar
or two, which was always an acceptable present, passed on through the
village towards the scene of the battle. Our guide Lambert, instead of
taking us along the main road towards Givonne, branched off a little to
the left after passing out of La Chapelle, and led us by a narrow road to
the top of a hill slope in order to point out the spot upon which two
Prussian batteries came into action against some few French flying
through La Chapelle, and from which the shells which had struck the
church and other buildings had been fired.

Though we afterwards saw many artillery positions of this kind, we saw none which struck us more than this. The wheel tracks left by the guns and limbers, the marks of the trail, the tops of a belt of young oak trees cut down by the gunners with axes in order to give a clear range, the exploded friction takes, pieces of wadding, &c., strewn about, and the fresh graves of horses, all enabled one to form a vivid picture of the batteries as they had stood in action upon the brow of the slope a few days before.

From this spot the village of Villars Cernay and Francheval could be seen in the low ground to our left front.

"From Villars Cernay," said our guide, "the Uhlans were first perceived as they came reconnoitring in that direction the evening before the battle;" and then he went on to tell us how he, in common with most of the neighbouring peasants, fled towards the forest on the approach of the German army,—that a French *Franc-tireur* fired at him as he was getting over a fence, and that several others were about to do so, when he called out "*La France!*" and managed to stop them just in time. "It was a great mistake," he said, "flying from the villages." His father, being an old man, chose to remain, and after the battle no damage was done to their house, the Germans only taking what was necessary for eating and drinking; but that when they found a house deserted by its owners and locked up, and thus no help or food to be got from it, they "smashed everything in it and did great damage."

After leaving the position of this battery we descended to Givonne, passing on our road some scattered French knapsacks and accoutrements, and crossing just before our entrance a little stream which flows through the village towards Bazeilles.

Givonne is a place of some size, built of substantial stone houses. One or two of them had been burnt to the ground by shells, but this seemed to have been the extent of the damage it had suffered.

A few Prussian infantry guarding some captured French waggons were in the streets, and the usual village life and bustle (it was market day) was going on around.

Recrossing the stream, we went on through Hayliés, which is a suburb of Givonne, and consists of a collection of manufactories, to Daigny, and from Daigny to La Moncelle. Up to this point we had seen comparatively few of the destructive traces of the battle, which, however, soon now became thick.

To eyes unaccustomed to the wreck of villages in war, the ruins of La Moncelle would be very striking. At this place there was a severe contest, and its streets as we passed through bore marks of it in rifle bullets, cartridges, French knapsacks, Prussian infantry helmets, water-bottles, and various other *debris* of the fight. Only two or three of its houses were left standing, the rest having been turned into mere blackened shells by the artillery fire of the contending troops. In the middle of the high road lay a large piece of a Prussian shell, and not far from it a soldier's postal ticket pierced by a bullet and stained with blood.

These tickets, called "*Field correspondentz-karte*," are issued to all soldiers, that they may write upon them home to their friends, and are very similar to our postal cards, the idea of which must have been borrowed from them.

In one of the most exposed parts of the village, and in the very midst of burnt and ruined houses, stands the church, untouched by a single bullet. In future ages the interposition of its patron saint ought, if the days are not too sceptical, to be believed in here, for nothing short of a miracle can, indeed, fairly account for its marvellous escape.

As one leaves La Moncelle, the road runs close to the little stream we have spoken of as flowing through Givonne to Bazeilles, and on each side of it the ground, smooth and cultivated, rises up to a much higher level by a tolerably gradual slope.

We mounted the height to our left hand (*i.e.*, to the east of La Moncelle), and walked along it to the village of Bazeilles. The remains of fires, with pieces of biscuit and pork scattered near them, and collections of broken bottles, most probably out of the pillaged wine caves of Bazeilles, showed that this plain had been the site of a bivouac. Lambert told us that it was a bivouac of *Franc-tireurs*; but we observed, generally, that everything either said, done, or suffered, by the French in the war, was always said to have been said, done, or suffered, by a *Franc-tireur*. They are the pet heroes of the villagers of France. The mixture of French and Prussian accoutrements, and French and Prussian cartridges (*chassepot*, needle-gun and *tabatière*), the carcases of horses still unburied, and the graves of men (marked simply by two little boughs tied together in the shape of a cross), showed also that the struggle for this part of the position was fierce and obstinate.

Close to Bazeilles, on the banks of the little stream, we came upon a heap of *mitrailleur* cartridge holders; each holder—square in shape—was of tin, covered with a sort of waterproof canvas, and with receptacles for twenty-five cartridges. The cartridges are turned by one motion out of these cases on to a plate opening into the breech of the gun, and then shut into the barrel.

Although we had never before seen these holders, there was no mistaking what they were, by anyone who had read the description of the engine with which Napoleon III. was going to overwhelm Germany.

Describing the assault of the ridge between Bazeilles and Daigny, the Prussian official account says:—

> A very violent artillery and *mitrailleur* fire led in the fight. The French took the offensive. General and vehement assaults were repulsed; at length the 23rd Division (of the 12th Corps) came up and took La Moncelle.

After spending some little time upon this ground, we entered what had once been the village of Bazeilles. So much has been written about the burning of this village—some of the houses of which were still smouldering—that it is unnecessary to describe it here. We can only say that nothing could exceed the completeness of the desolation and destruction of the spot.

Where some 3,000 inhabitants were living in their well-built stone houses, nothing remains hut a collection of skeleton walls and heaps of rubbish. Probably some 400 or more houses were destroyed, whether legitimately, according to the stern necessity of war, and in the hope of, by a terrible example, saving bloodshed in the end, or whether in the unjustifiable excess of cruelty, the verdict of history has yet to settle. As we passed into the village, a little mound of earth, in which was placed a stick with. a peasant's cap upon it, was seen. Two or three of the inhabitants, who escaped before the battle, still lingered among the scenes of their ruin, searching amidst the *debris*, and pouring out their grief and anger (there were no Prussians near) aloud.

The little cross, they said, marked the place where an inhabitant trying to escape had been shot; that some "*Franc-tireiurs*" (and not the inhabitants) had fired from the cellar rooms of the houses upon the Bavarian troops, and that on this account the village was set on fire, and every person, including innocent villagers, endeavouring to escape from it, was shot; and not this only, but that the day after the battle, the Bavarians returned to burn down the few remaining houses still standing, and led out several more peasants to be shot.

One woman with a child in her arms, which was crying (for want of food, she told us), and who brought us a cup of water out of the ruins of her cottage, was loud in her lamentations. "My husband," she said, giving a convulsive rock to still her child, "was an inoffensive villager, but was seized in the street by a Bavarian officer, who would have shot him had he not confessed where some stores in the village lay concealed; for this, his life was spared, but we are all ruined, all ruined."

Poor people, they were certainly in this battle passed under the harrow without mercy, and if future visitors to the spot are pestered beyond endurance—as from certain signs of our visit, even at the short interval after the battle, we believe they may be—by begging little boys holding boxes for "*les malheureux de Bazeilles*," let them, in memory of this certain truth, keep their patience, and perhaps give a few half-pence to them, if they are able.

To look upon the other side of the question, and in spite of the sufferings of the inhabitants of Bazeilles, it is not, we must remember, upon their statement alone that the guilt or otherwise of the burning of the village must be determined.

Many German officers, with whom we subsequently conversed, assured us that the inhabitants of Bazeilles, women as well as men, showed a vindictiveness that was most outrageously inhuman, not only shooting down the ambulance men and several Bavarian Soldiers, but attempting to drag the wounded into the burning houses; and a Prussian surgeon told us that if we wished we might interrogate a Bavarian officer under his hands, and able to speak, but almost at the point of death, from the effect of boiling oil which had been thrown upon him—this, of course, we did not do. The shooting of some peasants was admitted by some German officers, the firing the houses on the second day denied.

The *Franc-tireur*, or free rifleman, is a description of soldier with whom we never met, but the Germans describe him as being frequently dressed in an ordinary villager's blouse, with a belt sometimes over, but as often underneath it, and, in fact, as bearing no sort of certain mark of being anything but a peasant carrying a gun.

This renders it impossible, they say, for their own safety, to treat them as soldiers; as, if they did so, every armed peasant would call himself a *Franc-tireur*. As I have before said, we never met them; but from the German accounts they do not, at least did not at the beginning of the war, seem to correspond in any way (as I have seen urged occasionally) to citizens fighting in uniform, as English volunteers would for their homes.

One can understand how these *Franc-tireurs*, firing side by side with some of the peasants in the houses, may have helped to bring death and ruin upon innocent men.

All these points will be more fully and justly appreciated in the future; but one opinion, we should think, must always be entertained, and that is, that if the provocation to the Bavarians was great, their revenge was a relentless and bloody one.

We noticed that the village of Bazeilles was not in any way prepared for defence by loop-holing or cutting communications from house to house—*i. e.*, there were no signs of this on the skeleton walls. The defenders must have fired from doors and windows, and those who escaped did so, our guide said, by the back gardens and the fields along the Meuse. Marks of rifle-bullets were thick upon some of the faces of the houses still left standing, showing that the infantry fire must have been hot in the streets.

From Bazeilles we walked towards Balan, a neighbouring village and a sort of suburb of Sedan. The road between these two places, which is bounded by poplar trees, many of which were torn by shot, passes over an open country and is raised above the adjoining fields. On the right stretches the gently undulating plain west of La Moncelle, over which many of the retreating French were driven in rout, (and which we turned off to examine), and on the left large fields slope down towards the Meuse. These had been inundated to a great extent by the damming of the Meuse, which gave the country something the appearance of a lake. Near Balan, and close against the right bank of the road, we came again upon little heaps of *Mitrailleur* cartridge-holders, showing that here (where the raised road gave good natural cover) had been the position of some of these engines, the continuous growling of which in this direction is spoken of by most witnesses of the battle. Evidently, from the position of these *Mitrailleurs*, they had been directed against men who were attacking, after having come through Bazeilles, or round it, on the west. The inundated part of the Meuse could not be crossed.

Balan does not seem to have suffered much from the battle; but some iron shutters on a house on the right hand side as you enter had been struck and scored in long ridges by very many rifle-bullets, the ambulance flag hung out of several of the windows in Balan, and at the entrance of the village, close to the house with the scored shutters, was a large collection of arms taken on the field.

From Balan to Sedan is but a short distance, and there is not much of interest to detain one on the road.

We entered Sedan about sunset, having had full time, since we left La Chapelle in the morning, to examine very minutely every feature of the ground over which we passed. In fact, it would have been quite possible for us to have reached Sedan two or three hours earlier.

The appearance of Sedan very much surprised us. We had heard an account of its having been made a mass of ruins in the battle; and we confess that we had been, before seeing it, completely ignorant of its size and importance.

We were, therefore, a good deal astonished to find ourselves, after crossing the drawbridge of the fortifications and passing the German guard (who did not stop or question us) in the midst of a large town, with no marks of shot or shell visible in its streets, with well-lighted shops of many kinds—butchers' shops, with meat hanging up before the doors, and giving signs of plenty of food; confectioners' shops, libraries, hotels, restaurants—in short, all the usual shops lit up as brightly as one sees them on a quiet evening in peaceful times in some flourishing town.

Prussian soldiers were strolling through the streets, or making their purchases as quietly, and with as little appearance of being recent intruders as could well be conceived; and it was with difficulty, in spite of the presence of a few French wounded and the now familiar ambulance flag, that we could realize that near this town had been fought a few days previously one of the greatest battles of history, where an empire fell and 80,000 men had laid down their arms.

Certain notices placarded in the streets soon showed us, however, that we were far from being in an ordinarily governed town. Such were these:—

Sedan is proclaimed in a state of siege.

On any alarm in the night, no inhabitant, unless with authorization of the commandant, is to appear in the streets, and all are at once to light up their windows.

The captured and loaded arms will be fired off at 7 o'clock every evening in the fosse, so that this firing need cause no alarm.

Many other notices like these, giving instructions to the inhabitants and laying down pains and penalties, from fines up to death, met our eye, posted up sometimes, as if in irony, next to older proclamations still left standing, and which narrated some glorious but imaginary victory of the armies of MacMahon or Bazaine, and after which latter a satirical note of admiration in pencil could sometimes be detected.

Going to the ramparts to view the surrounding country, we asked a few questions of a German sentry who, with three medals on his breast, was pacing slowly up and down, and who seemed nothing loath to talk to us. It was very tiresome ("*Sehr langweilig*") being there, he said, and for his part he longed to get home to his family; for that their position in a conquered town was unpleasant for them and very unpleasant for Sedan.

This we could easily understand, for Sedan was, in fact, under martial law and at the mercy of the commandant of the 3,000 or so of Prussian soldiers of the *Landwehr* who formed its small garrison, and no one was admitted in or out of its gates after a certain hour. We tried in vain to obtain a lodging in the larger inns or hotels, and at last in despair attempted a little *auberge* in the Place Turenne called *L'Auberge de la Croix de Malte*, whose outside was not inviting. But one of those surprises so often met with in travelling was in store for us here, for we were made most comfortable inside, and found the people of the *auberge* (new arrivals in Sedan and full of apologies for their shortcomings), so civil and attentive, that we rejoiced over our rejection at the larger inns, and registered a vow that if we ever again came to Sedan we would go in gratitude to the *Croix de Malte*.

The next morning we reported ourselves to the commandant, who was out, but whose *aide-de-camp* gave us every information in his power, and at about eleven o'clock we set off with a guide to see the guns captured from the French, as well as those parts of the battlefield we had not as yet visited.

Going out from the town towards the suburb of Torcy, we crossed, by a stone bridge, the canal whose overflowing waters, had caused the inundation we spoke of near Balan and Bazeilles, and which extended slightly to this point also. Just inside the outer ramparts we came upon a trophy of war, I suppose hardly rivalled in history, consisting of some 400 field guns and 70 *mitrailleurs*, packed close together in a large open space. If it is considered that, in addition to this, some 100,000 *chassepots* are said to have fallen into the Germans' hands, the material gain of their triumph in this war (and this is saying nothing of what has since been taken at Metz) becomes apparent.

The German officers with whom we conversed all spoke in praise of the *chassepot*, as compared with their own needle-gun, though its bullet does not smash and kill so much. Its range is several hundred yards greater, a more important point, and it was not, they said, very improbable that they would, having taken; such a multitude of these weapons in the war, serve them out to their own army for future use.

The *mitrailleur,* or the French Montigny weapon, they have a poor opinion of, preferring, if they are obliged to take an engine of its size (that of an ordinary field gun and drawn like it by horses) out with them, to take a field gun at once, which, under four circumstances out of five, in a campaign is far more useful.

The *mitrailleur* they thought would be valuable for raking narrow roads or bridges and for protecting the ditches of fortresses, but its bullets are thrown in too great a shower together at close ranges, and thus are wasted—one man who is killed being probably pierced by several balls.

As we went out to, and returned from, this sight, waggons filled with rifles, collected on the field, kept passing us on the road, and we saw boys and men fishing for arms with poles and grappling irons in the canal and over the inundated ground on both sides of the bridge, now bringing up a sword, now a rifle, now a knapsack, and so on. The French soldiers had evidently thrown these into the water in their anger and rage when they were ordered to lay them down and capitulate.

Having seen the captured cannon, we retraced our steps, and issued this time from Sedan by the road leading towards Caval and Floing. Just after leaving the gates we were rather disagreeably confronted by a notice to the effect that anyone found wandering on the field of battle "*sans but*" (*i. e.* without some definite object), would be very heavily fined; but our guide told us that this was not enforced, and as we saw several idlers on the field afterwards, we imagine it was not.

We followed the road until close to the village of Floing, which lies almost hidden from view behind a spur or tongue of land stretching down from the wood of La Garonne towards the village and over-hanging it steeply.

We then turned off and ascended this spur (which we may call the Floing spur), as we knew that upon it one of the most severe struggles of the battle had gone on. The first thing which struck us on mount-ing a little way up it was the position (indicated by tracks upon the ground, and by the half-buried carcases of horses, their hoofs project-ing from the earth) of two French batteries, evidently the two alluded to by the War Correspondent of the *Pall Mall Gazette,* whose account of the battle we had read, as having been silenced by a Bavarian bat-tery from a hill near the village of La Villette. It was clear that these batteries, fully exposed as they were upon the hill .slope, would be at a great disadvantage in a duel with one properly concealed behind sloping ground; and our first thought was, why this French battery had not moved further back, so as to be on the reverse side of the ridge and sheltered by the crest?

It was in trying to find a reason for this, that we first became aware of how thoroughly the French on this spur were surrounded by the Germans on the morning of the 1st September; for on moving; over to the reverse, or northern side, of the spur, we found that this side also had been occupied by batteries—one placed immediately over the village of Floing and directed towards the village of St. Menges, about a mile off, and so situated that while it was defiladed by a steep wall-like dip in the ground close behind it from the reverse fire of the German guns near La Villette, it was from this circumstance—as the shells would strike and burst in the ground behind—placed in a sort of shell trap.

Also, from the downward slope of the ground, the gunners must have been fully exposed to the German batteries with which they were directly contending, and which had been drawn up behind a little *mamelon* near the corner of a wood in the direction of St. Menges (a little south of it.) This *mamelon* is described in some accounts as the "*Mamelon* of Floing." The earth torn up by shells, and two disabled gun-waggons left upon the ground, pierced and splintered, gave evidence of the sharp artillery duel at this point, which had been kept up from eleven until one o'clock.

The other battery was for *mitrailleurs*, six in number, a sort of rough gun pit having been dug for each *mitrailleur*.

The front of the battery faced towards the low and open ground beneath, in a direction between St. Menges and Illy, the earth being thrown up high on the left side of the pit, evidently to act as a traverse against flanking artillery fire from the direction of La Villette.

A wounded, melancholy-looking French soldier, who having lost his arm on this hill, had come again as soon as he could move about to see the spot where he had been struck down, pointed out to us the positions of the German batteries, and gave us some interesting particulars of the fight at this point. He, in common with all the French whom we spoke to, threw great blame upon their leaders, accusing them of "treason," and saying that all the superior officers were inefficient.

"One of our generals, he said, "was asleep in that little cottage over there, when they told him that the Prussians were moving round so as to enclose us; but he took no notice of it, and said it was all nonsense." "We heard a gun fired by the Prussians about 1.30 a. m., which was evidently the signal for their troops to march. There was no attempt to stop the enemy in crossing the Meuse, and no knowledge of the country. Our officers did nothing, and we were completely surprised."

The assertion as to treason is, we may confidently decide, groundless, and is too readily resorted to by the French; but the fact of the railway bridge over the Meuse, near Bazeilles, by which the Bavarians crossed, not having been destroyed is true, and the efforts which might have been made to retard the enemy in his passage of the river were certainly not made.

This wounded soldier said that he had remained three days lying upon the field, and mentioned also that some of the troops who fought in the battle had been taken from Floing as conscripts only two weeks before, and had no knowledge of their drill. He was soon joined by two or three other Frenchmen, "Our captain," said one, (an artilleryman belonging to the *mitrailleur* battery), "wouldn't believe that the troops marching round us were Prussians, and several times ordered us to cease fire, otherwise they would never have taken the hill."

"I saw them go down there," pointing to some little mounds of earth (graves) about 900 yards off in the valley, "by two hundred at a time," (evidently he exaggerated a little from pride in his weapon), "under the discharge of the battery, and up to ten o'clock we had good hopes (*bonne esperance*) that they would be beaten."

While talking to these soldiers and examining the position of this Floing spur with regard to the surrounding guns of the Germans, we saw that it would have been impossible for the French batteries to have been so placed upon it as to have been sheltered from reverse or enfilade fire. They were, in fact, taken at a heavy disadvantage.

After moving to the extreme edge of the spur, so as to see more closely the village of Floing (but without going down to it, as it had not suffered much in the battle), we walked up the spur in the direction of the woods at its summit, and past the little isolated red brick cottage where the French soldier said his general had lain asleep, our attention being turned more to the northern (or left hand) side, up which the German troops of the 11th Corps came to the assault. The slope is here of about 15°, smooth in most parts, except close above Floing, where it is broken and covered with bushes. Infantry could ascend it without difficulty, but to carry it under fire, even after its defenders had been shaken by a two hours' cannonading, must have required great pluck and determination.

Along the greater part of the ridge no attempt at intrenchments had been made by the French; but beyond the little red cottage—where the crest of the hill bends in the direction of Illy, so that from behind it a flanking fire can be brought across the northern slope up which the Germans attacked—commenced a line of entrenchment, which ran away in this direction for a distance of apparently some 500 yards.

It was the only example of shelter trench which we saw at Sedan. A well-directed army in good spirits could certainly have done far more, even in the short time, to strengthen this naturally strong, position (witness what was done by Meade's army on the night of the 1st June, 1863, before Gettysburg). It was very much of the form of the ordinary four feet wide and two feet deep shelter trench which the infantry soldiers of the English army are now taught to construct. Its defenders had evidently been shelled heavily, as numerous pieces of shell were met with here. Near the top of the Floing spur, and not very far from the woods, we saw several large gun pits, where the Germans had placed their guns of position, on the morning after the battle, in readiness to play upon the French in Sedan if their terms were not agreed to.

In the midst of all these signs of war one could see the first steps towards their obliteration, and the return to the old natural look of times of peace.

Sheep were cropping the grass near the shelter trench, and men were already at work filling in this and the gun pits, so that soon all trace of them will have passed away. We may mention that in no part of the field did we see batteries with embrasures, only hastily constructed sort of square pits, over the edge of which the guns fired "*en barbette.*"

Before ending our remarks upon what we saw upon the Floing spur, we ought to say that all along it, where the infantry fighting as well as the cavalry charges of the French had taken place, the ground was covered with the *debris* of the fight. The Prussian account says:—

At length the infantry took the ground about Floing, the enemy repeatedly charged it with cavalry. These charges, undertaken with wonderful bravery, in spite of the difficulty of the ground, were shattered and broken by the firmness of the infantry.

Cooking utensils pierced with bullets, packets of cartridges, helmets, accoutrements, soldiers' *livrets* (or small books), postal cards and letters, blown about by the wind, strewed the slope, and the graves of horses were frequent.

All the knapsacks that were met with in this day's wanderings were French.

The Germans had evidently collected all their own, and picked off also the brass ornaments of the helmets, leaving the leather portion (sodden and shapeless from wet, and often cut and disfigured) lying about the field.

Every French knapsack had been pillaged, and almost every cartridge emptied of its bullet, the powder being left and the load gone. "*Rien de tout—tout volé. Rien de tout—tout vole!*" was the constant and disappointed exclamation of our peasant guide, as with an irresistible impulse, which nothing could check (and which showed a good deal of the marauder in his composition) he kept turning over the cowhide packs with his long stick and heavy boots.

The spur descends at a gentle inclination from the wood above, and, except that it is somewhat rough, would not be unfavourable for the charge straight down it of a small body of cavalry; but on account of the narrowness of the spur, except high up near the wood, no extended line of horse could charge down it, and the slopes on either side are very unfavourable.

We picked up and read some of the letters blown about the field, partly with the hope that we might afterwards trace the writers of them, and return the letters to their families if any seemed of especial interest, and partly from curiosity. Generally, these letters alluded to accounts that had been received from the soldiers they were written to, of their despondency and misery.

Tell your companions, (said one), that they must not be discouraged; our district is even now raising another army, and we will drive the Prussians out of the country.

The following extracts we give in the original tongue, as well as in English:—

Nous avons reçu ta lettre, que nous a appris que tu es bien malleureux. Nous t'envoyons 10 francs pour diminuer un pen ta miser. Recommende toi toujours àla sainte Vierge. Elle tu pro egera pour nous. Nous le prions tons les jours.

Les details des fatigues que tu endures me poignardent le coeur. Que le grand Dieu du ciel daigne rejeter loin do toi, mon fils, les mauvais coups qui se preparent."

We have received your letter, from which we have learnt that you are very unhappy. We send you 10 *francs* to lessen slightly your wretchedness. Commend yourself always to the holy Virgin. She will protect you for us. Day by day we pray that it may be so.

The particulars of the hardships that you endure pierce my heart. May the great God of Heaven deign to keep far from you, my son, the evils that are in store.

After reaching the top of the spur, we passed straight on into a thick copse of beech and underwood, and just before we entered it came across a quantity of scattered music sheets, showing where a French band had lightened itself of the burden before plunging into the wood.

The "*Rhine Valse*" was marked on one of those we picked up. We issued from this wood close to a farmhouse, near which MacMahon is said to have been wounded.

A road towards Sedan runs past it, bounded on one side by a largish ditch, so that the story of the Marshal having been "left wounded in a roadside ditch," after vain attempts to retrieve his fortunes, may be possibly be founded upon fact. From this house we walked up the road in a northerly direction (away from Sedan), and soon came to a point where the wood on our left ceased, an open valley succeeding to it, while the wood ran on our right.

Along the valley a strong body of the French had evidently retreated, from the number of the knapsacks (principally belonging to the marines) strewing the ground.

It is the natural line which the defenders of the shelter trench, which we have alluded to, would have taken in endeavouring to escape towards Belgium; and from the little heaps of *mitrailleur* cartridge holders, it was evident that at all events one or two *mitrailleurs* had here come into action repeatedly—and often, owing to the undulations of the ground, at necessarily very short, ranges (say 200 yards or so)—to try and stem the torrent of the pursuit.

The edges of the wood on the right bore marks of the fight in broken and torn branches, but the interior would have been too thick for anything but a close hand to hand struggle, which we imagine there was no halt made for by the retreating troops.

After following the boundary of the wood for some distance, we entered it, passing by a mound of earth, from the surface of which glittered something, which our guide, who was in advance, stooped and seized, drawing out, before we could stay his hand, a sword bayonet, and pulling up its sheath and belt half out of the soil. Here then, just where he fell—on the very path itself—and with his accoutrements untouched, a few shovelfuls of earth had been thrown over the remains of some French soldier, whose dream in the morning had been perhaps of the glorious march to the Rhine, or of the marshal's baton, which, by tradition, his own and all the pillaged knapsacks of his companions, lying on this lost battlefield, held.

We replaced the sword, and after walking a few yards further, came into some open ground, where troops had bivouacked a very few days previously, and close to which stood the remains of a large, better class of country house or *chateau*, burnt to the ground.

Near it, several hundreds of the French, we were told, had laid down their arms; and in evidence of this, outside its walls we saw great heaps of cartridges, and many sets of accoutrements and knapsacks placed together in regular rows beside each other.

The destruction of this *chateau* was a striking evidence of the complete ruin caused by war. Walls burnt and blackened, furniture scattered in the yard (probably for defence) and destroyed—shrubberies trampled down, flower-beds torn up, fountains and statues broken and overturned—spoke mutely to the curse which lights upon those about whose fields and houses is fought out a deadly struggle such as this.

From the *chateau* we returned to Sedan by the high road leading past the citadel, which our guide said, on the evening of the battle, was strewn with horses and men, as the French fugitives (who, cut off from Belgium, endeavoured to get down it into Sedan) were taken at long range in front by the Prussian artillery from the heights far away in the direction of Wadelincourt, as well as fired into from the rear. The sides of this road were still thickly strewn with the signs of the rout.

We had now seen the field of battle well from the French positions, but wishing still to view it as it must have appeared to the Germans, we went out again next morning through Torcy, and so up to the height, about some two-and-a-half miles off, between the wood of La Marfée and the *chateau* of Donchéry, and above the village of Cheveuge, upon which, on a small potato field, the King of Prussia stood during the battle, and where he received the letter of Napoleon, saying, that unable to find death at the head of his army, he delivered up his sword.

The view from this hill is very extended, taking in a great portion of the entire field of battle, and, with the exception of parts towards and beyond Bazeilles and the northern slope of the Floing spur, we could trace from it with a glass almost all our wanderings of the previous days. Many points also, which could not be seen from the French positions, are here visible, including part of the course of the river Meuse.

Near Villette is seen a broken railway bridge, the only one which the French destroyed, and between it and Fresnois lies the *chateau* of Bellevue, where the Emperor had his interview with the Prussian King.

During the battle, columns of the German troops were drawn up in the low ground at the foot of the hill of Cheveuge, where the hollows and undulations afford (though it would hardly appear so from the summit of the hill) complete concealment from an enemy occupying, as the French did, the Floing spur and the high ground above Sedan.

We should imagine that the neighbourhood of a great battlefield could seldom offer a more perfect position than this from which—comparatively speaking, in safety—to watch the contest and to direct the movements of a large army; and to no one who has stood as we did upon these heights, and upon the spur above Floing (where the heavy guns of the Germans were placed the morning after the battle), can it be longer a matter of surprise why the French army, after their defeat and retreat into Sedan, surrendered as prisoners of war. It had no alternative, being caught as it were in a rat-trap, from which it could not hope to issue, and resistance in which would only have brought upon it a complete destruction.

After nearly an hour spent on this hill, we returned to Sedan, and as we did not like to leave the town without seeing for ourselves the ambulance of the Anglo-American Society, concerning whose charitable exertions we had heard so much, we walked up to the citadel, within the gates of which, in a large empty barrack, it had its quarters, and by permission of the surgeon went through the wards. Everything here seemed in most perfect order, the rooms airy and good; and as many of the less severely wounded had gone home, there was no overcrowding.

We believe that some of the surgeons of the ambulance, while dressing the wounded near this very spot on the afternoon of the fight, were themselves struck by pieces of shell fired from the German guns.

The town of Sedan, though under fire for some half-an-hour from the enemy's guns before the French, huddled together in its streets, offered to capitulate, bore but few traces of damage done. Shot marks on the Torcy gate and several other spots were to be seen, but that was all.

The scene of anarchy that its streets must have presented as the French army crowded into it under fire can be easily pictured, We were told by Madame Tellier, one of the principal booksellers of Sedan, that no words could express the sort of "pandemonium" that the place became. Before the battle even, it was, she said bad enough, for the troops had by that time lost heart and become discouraged by defeat.

From all we saw and heard at Sedan, we imagine, as we have before alluded to, that the French troops both began the fight on the 1st September without confidence in their leaders or themselves, and that as the day wore on, and they found themselves outnumbered and surrounded, this feeling of despondency rapidly increased into all abandonment of hope for, and every united aim at, success.

Desperate bravery was shown by individuals, and small bodies of men, but connected and well-directed efforts were wanting, and the tone and condition of the army was certainly, on the whole, bad.

CHAPTER 4

Sedan to Verdun

About three o'clock in the afternoon we left Sedan and set off towards Mouzon.

Our object was to reach the German army near Verdun, as we had been told by some officers at Sedan that there was a possibility of that place being shortly bombarded.

A battery of guns captured at Sedan had been sent to the force around Verdun, and as at Mézières and Montmédy nothing very active was looked forward to, it appeared our best course to try and gain Verdun, and perhaps afterwards pass on to Metz.

All our efforts to obtain any kind of conveyance had failed, for every cart and horse was in requisition for the transport of the wounded, or for bringing in arms from the field of battle, and on the commandant's advice we set off on foot, trusting to being able to procure some kind of vehicle further from the scene of the great tight.

Time being an object to us, made us grudge every delay caused by this slow mode of travelling; but had it not been for this, no one could have desired a more pleasant way of moving over the country in the perfect weather which we were fortunate enough to enjoy.

On our road today we entered into conversation with a French peasant, who, on hearing that we were Englishmen, told us that he had just seen a stone cross near Balan which was to be put up to the memory of some English officer, who had been killed in the Battle of Sedan.

Possibly this now marks the spot where the much-regretted Colonel Pemberton fell, but whose body we were glad to see has been borne to an English home.

This officer, formerly in the Grenadier Guards, was killed by a French rifleman while acting as War Correspondent to the *Times* with

141

the German army, his desire to see the action having led him too far into the fight.

It was nearly six o'clock before (*via* Bazeilles and Douzy) we arrived at Mouzon, a large town with a fine cathedral in it, and entered a little inn called the *Hotel de Commerce*, one of the first houses of the place.

It was at Mouzon that MacMahon was driven with such loss over the Meuse on the 30th of August, and like Sedan, it was occupied by a German garrison, and was in a state of siege, no one being allowed in the streets after 9 p. m. To our request for something to eat, the landlady replied, rather to our surprise, that there was "*a table d'hôte;*" and before long we found ourselves seated at this, surrounded by surgeons of all nationalities—Belgian, German, French and English, bearing the red cross and at work with various ambulances—and by three or four private gentlemen of rank travelling to see wounded friends, among them a near relative (son or nephew) of Count Bismarck.

In one of the English surgeons we met a Mr. Turner, an ex-combatant officer of the army, who knew many friends of ours in Canada (where he had served with the 47th Regt.), as well as in other parts of the world, and who gave us much interesting information about the war. He spoke in high terms of the cheerfulness of the Prussian officers and soldiers under the privations which they had gone through in wet weather after the Battle of Sedan, and of their fortitude under pain. To our question as to whether this was not equally the case with the French soldiers, he replied, "He ought not to say, as he had attended comparatively few of them, but that by nature the Germans seemed to be very peculiarly stoical under suffering."

He also dwelt strongly upon the perfect organization with which the German volunteer civilian societies—Saxon, Bavarian, Wurtemburgian, &c,—formed themselves into bodies for the service of the wounded, and of the good work done generally by the Volunteer Association of the Johanniter, or Knights of St. John. This society is composed almost entirely of members of good German families, and we saw several combatant officers on active duty with the army wearing the cross of the order, which is highly thought of. Their assistance, we suppose, was principally confined to money aid.

It was a pleasure to us to listen to a Prussian surgeon speak in high praise of the exertions of the English and Anglo-American Ambulance Society, saying that it was very efficient, and did hard and zealous work, rendering great service to the wounded of both nations. No doubt, among the many who have donned the red cross in this war, there are some who have done so for pure convenience of travelling, (for the red cross passes, or use to pass, freely,) and some for even more unworthy motives; but the badge has certainly won itself admiration and respect on the whole.

From our medical companions we learnt, also, that the French wounded were generally shot in the middle of the body or back, the Germans high up in the body, the tendency of the French being to fire high; and that men recovered very quickly from the wounds of the *chassepot* bullet.

It was at Mouzon that the Bavarian officer, mentioned before as said to be suffering under the boiling oil thrown on him at Bazeilles, was stated to be lying.

One thing which struck us much in this place, and which had been gradually forcing itself upon us since we left Belgium, was the absence of all news from the seat of war. People knew less than we did—fresh as we were from London and the *Times*—of the more recent events of the campaign.

Letters were, we were told, rarely received. A Dutch surgeon had been five weeks without hearing from his wife in Holland, and Mr. Turner had been almost an equally long time without, news from England; the reason given for this was that the Field-post, though it could be used to take letters out from those with the army, was not always to be counted upon to bring letters in.

The inhabitants of the villages were completely ignorant of what was going on. They had all been told (probably as a matter of policy by the Germans) of the French disaster of Sedan; but beyond this they were perfectly in the dark as to where the French armies were, and many of them talked as if they expected that their villages might be at any moment retaken by the French generals, whom they imagined to be close in the neighbourhood.

There is nothing, of course, in the least unaccountable in all this, for the machinery of special correspondents, and telegrams and news-papers, is not employed for the benefit of the residents, of Sedan or Mouzon, as it is for those of London; but it struck one as strange that the knowledge of events should be so very much less among all classes nearer the theatre of their occurrence, than at miles away from it in another land.

The poor landlady of the *Hotel de Commerce* seemed to have adopt-ed one formula in answer to a request for anything, except what she had set out upon the *table d'hôte*, *"Monsieur, les Prussiens ont tout pris;"* and she gave it out to us even when we applied for the key which was wanting in the bedroom lock.

At Mouzon we tried hard, as at Sedan, to get a conveyance, but here again everybody's horse and cart seemed in requisition.

One of the surgeons told us he could have *given* us a horse (one of two or three which he had got, and of which any number could be picked up for the taking and feeding after the surrender at Sedan), but that he had already offered it as payment to a villager for carrying a parcel for him to Douchéry, for he was going away soon from Mouzon and would not require the animal, the last he had kept, any more.

This incident struck us as being curiously characteristic of the exceptional state of things produced by the war.

Failing in all private attempts to get a vehicle or animal of any description, we went to the commandant to see if he could aid us.

Here we suffered for the sins of another, for we were told that it was entirely out of his power to grant conveyances, more especially as he had done so to one who had letters from the English Ambassador, Count Bernstoff, and who came from England, and now five days had elapsed, and his cart and horse had never been returned. Fortunately, as one of us knew the name of this offender, we were able to convince the commandant that he was, at all events not an Englishman, but an ex-Prussian officer, who had lived some time in England, and his threats of imprisonment for him, if he ever caught him, on hearing this, were very amusing.

We failed, therefore, in getting a conveyance; and with the exception of a lift of two miles or so, upon a little donkey cart, kindly given to us by a good-natured Swiss surgeon, who turned back a little for the purpose, and who had "picked it up" in some manner, we walked on to Stenay, where we arrived about mid-day. Our kind driver was very amusing in his conversation. "Ah!" he said, "battles are nasty things! Just because I knew languages, my chief said to me, 'Here, you go in front under fire; because you can speak, if they make a mistake and are going to shoot at you;' so I had to go, and one big Prussian, who could not see the cross on my arm, was just going to fire when I called out to him—and then the shells coming *'phut,' 'phut!'*—Ah! *ce n'etait pas joli du tout, du tout!"*

"Now," he said (encouragingly), "I must turn back here.

The country is full of robbers; it's a fine time for them, and no one cares whether you're murdered or not, if you ain't a Prussian."

Our road today lay through the villages of Moulins, Inor and Martincourt, and over a lovely country. Long stretches of meadow land bordered the Meuse, dotted over here and there with grazing cattle, and on each side of us spread away a succession of sweeping hills, deeply wooded,—from the nooks and valleys among which peeped out the church spires of red tiled and picturesque French villages. But these villages, though they pleased the eye at a distance under the bright morning sun, were dreary and deserted-looking enough when yon entered their streets. Half the inhabitants had left their houses and fled; and as we passed through Martincourt, a wretched-looking being, finding we were English, asked if we thought he could obtain employment as a wood-turner in England, his occupation being gone, and he and his family being at the point of starvation in Martincourt.

We noticed that the telegraph wires along the road today bore marks of having been cut and replaced again in very many parts.

On entering Stenay, which is an open town of some size, we saw a detachment of the 4th German Hussars just come in from before Verdun. This detachment, wearing a sort of dark, chocolate coloured uniform, with tight breeches and butcher boots, and mounted on small horses in good condition, had the look of thoroughly workmanlike campaigners, though their appointments had none of the polish that we get in time of peace in England. They carry a breech-loading carbine, strapped to the saddle after our old clumsy fashion. But they were lighter in appearance than the Uhlans (Lancers), who are as heavily equipped as any English Lancer regiment, and carry a more clumsy lance—and a great contrast to the Prussian heavy cavalry, whose large *cuirasses*, and pot helmets, and heavy boots, worn much as in Charles I. time, give them exactly the look of the dragoons of Cromwell, as shown in the pictures of that period.

While upon the subject of the Prussian Cavalry, which arm has been made so much use of, and worked so well in this war, we may mention that we gathered in conversation with officers the following particulars, which may be of interest to soldiers:—

The *Cuirassiers*, or Heavy Cavalrymen, assert that their *cuirass* turns the French *chassepot* bullet—*i.e.*, causes it to glance off—and that it is beyond doubt of great defensive value.

The kit carried by the Uhlan consists of a *shabraque*, blanket, shirt, one pair of socks, a forage cap, and a pair of slippers, (the latter often placed in the right holster). In addition to this kit the man, of course, has the uniform he sits in. His arms are lance, sword and pistol, and he often carries with him one day's provision of corn.

The men place the blanket (which, while useful as such, stands in lieu of our *numnah*) next the horse's back, the saddle over it, and often between the saddle and the *shabraque* a suit of linen slop clothes for dirty work,—the *shabraque*, a light cloth one, going over all, and, of course, giving a better appearance to the turn-out. Three or four waggons go with each squadron, and carry spare things and horse shoes for each horse.

We know that cavalrymen in our service assert that the blanket, unless very carefully folded, rucks up and gives sore backs to the horses; but the Prussian Cavalry saddle is light and well raised off the backbone, and the Prussians stated that it and the blanket worked very satisfactorily. The girths to the Prussian saddle are made of twisted leather.

The Uhlans wear, at all events those of them we saw, strapped overalls as do our lancers, not breeches short like their own Hussars, or loose trowers tucked into the boots like the Austrian Uhlans.

The Hussar dress—putting arms (*i. e.*, the lance and its pennon) on one side, and speaking only of clothing,—if it be not the best, as many think it is, is beyond all doubt the most effective, and at the same time most workmanlike in appearance. We have never seen a horseman who realized our *beau ideal* of the Cavalier so completely as a keen-eyed Hussar officer who passed us one day well-mounted on the road near Metz in his chocolate coloured uniform, tight breeches and Hessian boots, covered with dust, and with a long straightish-shaped sword, hanging rapier-like by his side. He and his horse seemed alike full of the activity and dash which should mark cavalry, and both would have been fitting figures in a picture of the glittering and attractive side of "glorious war."

We believe that the German Hussar regiments are entitled to a good deal of the exceptional renown gained by the Uhlans as reconnoiterers in the war, one half of the work having been done by them, but the glory having fastened itself to the attractive pennon of the lancer. Every German cavalry soldier was at first dubbed by the French an "Uhlan," and so the name became very generally misapplied.

Almost all the German troopers we met with were intelligent in appearance, though by no means more so than those of an English regiment, and their horses were in good condition. One could not, of course, tell the number on the sick list.

Outpost work and reconnoitring are the duties most studied and attended to by them. Charges certainly have been made in the war (as a rule in open column of squadrons) but with frightful destruction to the cavalry.

The revolver buckled round the waists of some of the officers in Stenay, and which one only sees (with English officers at all events) when pretty close to an enemy, helped us to realize that we were drawing near now to the theatre of active hostilities. A Prussian company (250 men or so) garrisoned Stenay, which is within some ten miles of the French fortress of Montmédy.

The commandment was most civil to us, giving us a pass to travel further, assisting us in the difficult job of finding a conveyance, and pointing out our best route upon the maps in his office. I have since been very sorry to hear of his fate, which was that of being surprised, a few nights after our visit, by a sortie from Montmédy, when he and all his followers were made prisoners by the French. In conversation with us the officers at Stenay spoke of the garrison of Montmédy as consisting of "only a few Mobiles;" and I fancy an undue contempt for it, combined with a foggy night, were the causes of their rather humiliating fate.

Even with the commandant's assistance, it was no easy matter to find an unemployed conveyance in Stenay. A member of the first family to whom we went appealed to us imploringly with "My horse is now away, but I and my mother are here alone; how *can* I go with you?" and we were obliged to search a good deal before we secured one. During this search we came across two of the most hospitable peasant families that we have ever met with in any country. One of the heads of these, a jolly sort of old woodman living in a very humble, little cottage, insisted, on opening for us two bottles of different descriptions of *très bon vin*, while he sent his son to try and find a friend's cart for us.

The son speedily returned with an exceedingly pretty girl, who had been a lady's maid in Paris, and unlearnt village manners long since, and she conducted us to her father's house. Here, after sitting for some time eating grapes and offering in exchange our chocolate and cigars, and discussing the events of the war, we agreed with a son of the house to drive us to Bras, a German post before Verdun. The difficulty was to settle upon a route. The commandant had told us to take a round about one by Buzancy and Grand Prè as safer from any chance robber or *Franc-tireur*; but the French peasant pointed out that

147

this was seventeen kilometres—*i. e.*, half a day's journey—longer than the direct one by Sivry, and that we, driven by a Frenchman and in plain clothes, had nothing to fear. Want of time and the honest look of the driver made us settle upon his plan, and we agreed to sleep at Sivry that night.

Our French hosts at Stenay did not appear to have suffered much from the war, though they were very decided in their expressions of the misery it was causing generally, especially to the agricultural classes and to owners of cattle. The woodman spoke well of the Germans individually, but was candid enough to say, (the strongest expression I heard used on my travels,) that he hoped "they would never get back to their own country."

Having experienced great kindness from both Germans and French in Stenay, we drove out of its gates between the two sentries (who carefully examined our passes) with feelings so perfectly balanced, that we were, I think, (as we ought to have been,) "impartial neutrals," rather given, perhaps, to moralize upon the fully of war in general. I have often thought since of how the old woodman must have rejoiced over that surprise of the German garrison, and can see him now cracking another bottle of his *très bon vin* to celebrate the event.

Our drive of this afternoon led us through the villages of Mouzay and Dun, to Sivry, about fifteen miles.

We have said before that most of the villages between Mouzon and Stenay had appeared desolate to us, but those on our road today seemed to out-desolate their desolation, and Sivry was the most melancholy and forlorn of all. The cattle disease was raging here, and had combined with the war to ruin the little village, the neighbourhood of which, one would think, must be always lonely and deserted, as a cross close to the entrance marks the spot where an old woman, in November of 1869, had been devoured alive by a hungry wolf.

Scarcely a human being was to be seen in the dirty—filthily dirty—streets, and anything more suggestive of an abandoned, plague-stricken spot can hardly be imagined. There are three places which, from their dreary, ruined look, have impressed themselves above all others upon our minds during our life time—Cawnpore[1], after the massacre and the sacking of the bungalows; Bazeilles, near Sedan, and Sivry. The little *auberge* where we put up for the night, and which had its sign

---

1. *The Cawnpore Man: A First Hand Account of the Siege and Massacre During the Indian Mutiny By One of Four Survivors* Mowbray Thompson also published by Leonaur.

removed in the hopes of escaping Prussian visitors—who the landlady told us, had on a former occasion cleared her out of everything, one soldier finally nourishing a bayonet and forcing her to show him to the cellar in order to get her best wine—was uninviting enough outside, but inside we were made fairly comfortable.

The woman of the house spoke both discontentedly and very despondingly of her own prospects and of those of her village. One son was shut up in Verdun, from the direction of which place cannonading had been heard throughout that morning; another was in Montmédy. Her cattle had all died of the disease which was raging there, and she looked forward with certainty to the approaching visits of typhus and cholera, and other plagues bred by the poisoned air. In short, of all the French villagers we had met with, she seemed to be the one who had felt the war as a personal calamity the most.

A lean pointer dog and a hungry cat, which mewed to us for food, shared the dinner with us; and after sitting for half-an-hour round the kitchen fire with the keeper of the *auberge*, the landlady, our driver, and a dark-looking man, who appeared from we knew not where, and discussing the general misery caused by the war, we went upstairs to our bedroom in anything but a buoyant or cheerful frame of mind, one of the last questions which the landlady sent after us being, if we meant "to return that way," followed by a scolding injunction, as we touched the handle of a wrong door, not to "enter any other room but our own."

When once in the latter we were soon asleep, but were not destined to enjoy a very peaceful night of it. About twelve one of us awoke, and not liking the sounds which came at this time from the lower part of the house, called to the other, who proved to be awake also, and to have liked them still less.

Our discussion of these noises and the plan of action we adopted on account of them, make us smile now; but at the time we felt in a very serious and anxious mood indeed, and though the story we are about to tell may raise a laugh against ourselves, we will relate it.

The possibility of our being in evil quarters flashed upon us. All the tales we had read of murders in Spanish and Pyrenean inns, of descending smothering beds, of missing travellers found buried under floors, and of the evil character given by the Prussians to some of the French peasantry, flashed through the mind.

We now saw how tempting a prize we must appear to any lawless men. We were evidently not Prussians, and therefore not likely to be enquired after, had money with us (for had we not agreed to pay a good sum for a conveyance?), and to all appearance (and we knew it to be the case ourselves) were without arms. Everything looked suspicious. Had the people at Stenay been civil to us only to induce as to go to Sivry? Was the driver in league with the inn-keeper? Why had the strange-looking man come in? Was there anything concealed in the room, the door of which we were so scolded for touching? And finally why were they up at so late an hour?

Not being able to answer these questions satisfactorily, we got up, silently dressed by the moonlight, and prepared as far as we could for an emergency. To barricade the door well (though we did so slightly) was impossible. To fight our way downstairs and out, unarmed, and past three or four (perhaps knife-bearing) people, looked, though it was mooted, to be foolish bravery, so at last we resolved, as a final resort, and if the door was attempted, to drop from the window, some ten feet or so, into the street, and make for the Prussians towards Dun.

All we can say to those who laugh at us, is, "May you never fancy yourselves in a like predicament!"

How the noises had stopped when we talked,—how we lay awake from twelve o'clock till dawn—how once again they were renewed and again ceased,—how, finally, steps were heard coming up the stairs, which, on our showing unmistakeably that we were awake, paused and came no further, would not be interesting if described at length.

Suffice it to say, that we welcomed the dawn, and that we believed that we experienced two-thirds of the perhaps exciting, but most unpleasant sensations, of the individuals whose tales of escape from Spanish and Pyrenean inns we have before alluded to.

The next morning the landlady enquired how we had slept, and whether we would "return that way?" We said "perhaps," but inwardly determined that we never should; and though we are willing now to believe that our imaginations made fools of both of us that night, we resolved to stick in future to Prussian posts, and to the advice of their commandants, and were not sorry to say goodbye at length to Sivry.

About eight o'clock we set out again in our waggon for Bras, one of the outposts of the Prussian force that was blockading the town and fortress of Verdun. As during yesterday's journey, so upon today's also, all the little villages on the road appeared abandoned and desolate, and much distress had' evidently been caused by the disease among the cattle.

A company of foot artillery (probably going to Sedan) passed by us this morning, their knapsacks and accoutrements, we noticed, being carried for them in waggons; and from one of the officers we heard that there had been a sortie from Verdun the day previously, which had been repulsed with slight loss, and hence the cannonade which had reached the ears of the landlady at Sivry. A two hours' drive, principally up hill, brought us to Bras, where we called to report ourselves to Major Von Dobschütz, the commandant.

At this point, before going on our visit to the Germans near Verdun, we hope it will not be thought tedious if we give our impressions (gathered through our whole trip from Sedan to Metz) of the feeling of the peasantry in general towards those whom the fortune of war had brought to them as uninvited guests; and an account of the Prussian system of requisitions—which is that followed by the whole German army—by which they obtained their supplies and transports in the various villages. Some misapprehension we think exists in many quarters on these subjects.

To begin with, we must say that in all the villages, without exception, through which we passed, the people did, reluctantly but invariably, admit that the German soldiers and officers conducted themselves well as a rule. We heard no abuse of the Germans as individuals. The tale of the landlady at Sivry, of the bayonet having been flourished at her, (and it must be remembered that the violence went no further) was the worst we had related to us. The usual phrase was "*Non, Monsieur, ils sont assez gentils!*"

That great suffering is, and will be, the result of the German occupation and of the war, in consequence both of the consumption of food and forage, and the withdrawal of almost all the active men and the boasts of burden from the tillage of the soil, is very certain; but, at all events, this evil did not appear to have been aggravated in any of the occupied districts we saw by wanton brutality or even by bullying language.

The manner of the German officers, though that of masters who meant to have their way, was always, as far as we observed it, rather markedly courteous. It would appear from the statements subsequently received from the seat of war around Paris, that this was not true of the Germans in that quarter, but we only speak of what we saw with our own eyes, and heard on the spot in Lorraine; and the peasantry, it must be remembered, when told that we were English, were never reticent.

The expressions of "*Ils ont tout pris,*" "*Ils ont pillé par tout,*" so very common, referred to the eatables and drinkables of life, and to horses; and the German army system bore very hardly, as we will explain further on, upon the villagers in these respects, but their misery was ascribed invariably not to their visitors, the Germans (whom we often saw playing with and nursing their children,) but to "*la guerre.*"

The people of Lorraine were, as a rule, (the old *Garde de Chasse* at Stenay was an exception) seemingly indifferent as to whether the Germans went or staid, provided they had "*la tranquilite.*"

"*Ma foi!*" was the usual burden of their answer to our questions regarding their feelings at the prospect of annexation to Prussia, "*Qu' est que c'est le Gouvernement à moi? Je suis ouvrier; je désire seulement la paix;*" or, "*Ma foi! qu' est que c'est à moi se je suis Français ou si je suis Allemand?*" &c.

The bitterness of the language of the peasantry seemed entirely directed against the much abused Napoleon III. "*Quand j'ai vu cette malheureuse famille* (*i.e.* the Emperor and his son) *entrer dans notre ville,*" said a woman to us in Sedan, "*j' ai dit 'maintenant nous sommes perdus.'*"

One is, of course, well aware of the little weight or importance that should be attached to sayings like the above. It is easy to understand how the ground-down peasant, who shares none of the glory, but pays the penalty of war, may feel such a longing aspiration after "*la tranquilité,*" even at the price of becoming a German, though he is a Frenchman at heart, and at the first sign of weakness or reverse on the part of his enemy would rise and crush him without mercy; and we also understand how very loudly those of the French who now abuse Napoleon III. and call him the sole originator of this war would have asserted their boundless admiration both for his person and his policy had he been successful; yet, with all this, the result of the many conversations which we held on our journeys among the peasantry in the Ardennes and Lorraine, was to convince us that the people in this part of the country would put up with a just and orderly German government far more cheerfully than people in England would be inclined to believe, and that after some years of such a firm and unoppressive government the enthusiasm necessary for a patriotic rising against German occupation would he sought for in vain.

With regard to the German method of payment for their supplies, we had our preconceived ideas much altered. It is common to hear the remark that the Germans "pay in paper" for what they take, or that they "give an acknowledgment on paper which is binding on the government," &c., and we are tolerably certain that a very common impression in England is that this paper pledges the German government to hand that peasant, or the village official who represents him, in cash, at some future time, the value of what was taken from him. Nothing is more erroneous than this idea, and no system of payment could well be devised which would carry out the First Napoleon's theory that "*War should support war*" (without exasperating more than is unavoidable the inhabitants of a country) more thoroughly than does the German one.

The German requisition is made for all necessary carriage, forage, food, tobacco and wine for men and officers, the scale of which is laid down by authority, and is a liberal one. The paper is merely an acknowledgment to the mayor of a village, or other official, through whom the supplies are got, that they in reality were got, and *if* the government of France chooses in the future to reimburse the people for what they have lost, through no fault of their own, but through the fortune of war, these requisitions will enable the right sums to be apportioned out to the mayors, &c., of the villages, and through them to the villagers.

This, however, it can be at once seen, is a very different; thing from "payment for all supplies" as it is understood and practised in war in the British Service, and, in fact, binds the German government to nothing at all.

The villagers as a rule do not quite grasp this, and to obtain a formal piece of paper acknowledging the supplies looks like the probability of payment, and is far more satisfactory than no paper at all. Very probably, indeed, the French government would in any case consider these requisitions as debts of honour, and will redeem them; but from what source is the money which is to do this to come, except from a tax on the nation, of which these very villagers will pay their share.

But as we have said above, it is only for carriage and the reasonable maintenance of man and beast that these paper acknowledgments are given. For all extra luxuries the individuals who obtain them must pay in cash, and any attempt at oppression or unfair dealing would meet with a prompt punishment. The German authorities deal very severely with grave offences against the inhabitants. We were told by an inhabitant of Sedan that a soldier had been shot a few days previous to our visit for stealing a watch. Thus in all private dealings in which officers or soldiers come into personal contact with the villagers, the usual payments (at ordinary rates) arc made, the relative value of German and French money being posted up conspicuously throughout the villages by the German authorities.

Now, by reflection upon this system of payment, it can be seen that though the German government in reality pays, and binds itself to pay, nothing to the French for the food and transport of the army, it deals in these matters with the villagers indirectly (*i. e.* through the *maire* or French official), and gives to him a paper acknowledgment, which may some day, at the end of the war, be to the peasant worth something; and that, on the other hand, where any direct relation between its soldiery and the individual villagers takes place, it insists upon cash, and the correct sum in cash, being given.

It would be, we think, difficult to devise a system combining practical economy, with the advantages of conciliating the population dealt with, more than this does. We are not sure that, though a hard and ungenerous system, it can be termed an unfair one.

The English government pays for everything in war, even though the war be forced upon it, and does so at an enormous expense to the English people; and yet why should the English people be out of pocket more than the people of the country causing the war.

The French pay for nothing (at least so it is generally asserted of them by those who have served with them), and thus make bitter enemies of the inhabitants of the countries they make war on.

The Germans, as far as possible, hit the medium between the two extremes.

We should be sorry though, for all this, to see the English system changed, for it is a generous and noble one; and under any other, the peasantry of a country—who, as a rule, have but little to do with causing wars—must suffer for a time more grievously than any subsequent payment can make up for. In a long war, also, (if the days of long ones are not past) the English practice will prevail, as it gains the goodwill of the inhabitants.

CHAPTER 5

Verdun—Its Bombardment

The commandant at Bras gave us not only a courteous, but a most friendly reception, and at our request, after having asked some questions to satisfy himself as to our trustworthy character, permitted us to visit the advanced posts and sentries on the heights of Belleville, accompanied by one of his officers, who volunteered most kindly to do everything in his power to show us all that was of interest.

The Germans immediately around Verdun were distributed among the villages of Bras, Fleury, Eix, Vaux, &c., and had, up to the day before our arrival, been in insufficient strength to entirely close all access to the town, but a small force having just arrived, it was now completely surrounded.

Our guide, a Staff officer, rode by our side for about one-and-a half miles out of Bras along the Verdun road. If one follows this road for about that distance, one will see a small copse of wood to the right, just where the road begins to descend towards Verdun. Here one of the German pickets was placed, but before coming to it we turned off to the left into a country path, and, after making a detour of some distance and keeping in the low ground to avoid observation, we came to another picket, to which our guide entrusted his horse, remarking that we were now within short cannon range of the enemy's guns, and that the French, who had plenty of ammunition and signalmen on the lookout in the cathedral tower, invariably sent a shell after any one, especially on horseback, who exposed himself.

Then turning into a thick copse of low beech trees, he led us through it to its further edge, which lined the crest of one of the hills on the plateau of Belleville overlooking the valley of the Meuse. Here partially parting the branches and carefully placing his sword on one side to guard against its glitter being seen, he showed us Verdun lying

155

at our feet. The nearest bastion of the fortress could hardly have been more than 1,500 yards distant, and six feet from the spot where we stood was a large gap rent in the earth by the explosion of a shell. With a field-glass we had a distinct view of all the buildings of the town. Dominating the whole ran the high double tower of an old Norman Cathedral, upon which the French sentries were to be seen holding flags for signalling in their hands.

More to the right stood the citadel; between us and the body of the town came part of the outer circle of fortifications, on Vauban's system, with its bastions and curtains and broad ditches; and nearer than all wound the River Meuse, the railway bridge over which had been rendered impassable by blowing up the arch nearest to the works.

Verdun[1], lying as it does in low ground surrounded by hills, must always at the present day be at the mercy of an enemy provided with siege artillery.

The Germans, however, had no guns of greater calibre than the six-pounder Krüpp breech-loading held gun used in their own service, and a battery of French twelve-pounder field gun captured at Sedan, just arrived, and whose departure from the latter place we have before mentioned that we had been informed of.

These batteries would, it is to be noticed, correspond respectively to about twelve and twenty-six (or perhaps heavier guns in the English service; for the Germans and French name their artillery in pounds by what would be the weight of a spherical shot of the diameter of the bore, whereas we name it by the weight of the heavy elongated projectile really used. Thus their guns may be considered as being in truth doubly as formidable as guns called by the same number in the English army.

The artillery of the fortress of Verdun was formidable enough easily to overpower the six-pounder guns at any range at which the latter could do much damage to the works, and the French twelve-pounders having only recently been received, no bombardment had as yet been attempted, the active hostilities being confined to the repulse of an occasional sortie, and intermittent firing to harass the German posts.

The sentries on the cathedral tower were a source of great annoyance to the Germans, as they were continually on the alert, and from their elevated position were able to see and direct shells to be fired upon patrols, &c., that would otherwise have escaped observation.

1. *'Neath Verdun: the Experiences of a French Soldier During the Early Months of the First World War* by Maurice Genevoix also published by Leonaur.

With the exception of these sentries and the occasional glitter of steel (suggestive of a bayonet) appearing along the ramparts, there was nothing in the town which indicated the presence of human life, and for some time not a sound breaking the extreme stillness of the day arose from its streets. At length the report of a cannon fired towards a German outpost on the side opposite to us boomed upon the air, but there was no answer to the shot, and the silence once again reigned unbroken.

To gaze upon this beleaguered town had to us a sort of fascination in it difficult perhaps to explain, but which we confess to having felt. Apparently asleep or dead, we knew it to be instinct with a watchful and dangerous life, and though its ramparts, and walls, and buildings, must have borne much the same look as they had done in peaceful times, the imagination helped to clothe them with one entirely different. We stood for some time looking down upon the quiet town, carful lest by a breaking twig or crackling leaf we should arouse it from its slumber, and, cause it to cry out wrathfully at us from the black mouths of the cannon pointing in menace from the embrasures. Then going quietly back, we were led by our guide to many other points where we could obtain different views, and finally—after a visit to some of the advanced sentries, and to the infantry and cavalry pickets, which we came upon unexpectedly round the corner of a wood or in some dip in the hills—by the road we had originally come over, buck to Bras.

Here we dined with the commandant and one of his officers in their billet in the Mairie, and afterwards had coffee and a very pleasant hour's conversation with the officer commanding; the field battery. We had, while at dinner, an example of the unnecessary obsequiousness of the French Mayors, and of the curious combination of accomplishments that may be found in a *Landwehr* soldier. Coming in, napkin in hand, to see if we were all well served, the Mayor took occasion to say that neither France nor England were now the great countries of the world, but Prussia. "Though I am a Frenchman, I say, gentlemen, that the greatest country in the world is Prussia." This he said twice.

There was no occasion for his making the remark at all; this is the only fault we are finding with it.

The *Landwehr* corporal, whose accomplishments we have spoken of, was a gigantic German, about 6 feet 5 inches in height, and who I suppose was a known character to his officers; for on his being asked, evidently to elicit a certain answer, what he was by occupation? he replied, with a laugh, "Formerly teacher of Mathematics, afterwards Professor of Natural Philosophy, and now corporal in the *Landwehr.*"

The officers here told us that at the village of Charny, close to and visible from Bras, two German *cuirassier* officers had been murdered not long before. They had ridden into the town and dismounted at an inn for breakfast, but on trying to leave the village, a mob collected and demanded their surrender. Refusing to yield, they endeavoured to cut their way through the mob, and were both killed.

"They said," went on our informant, that "the *Franc-tireurs*, and not the villagers killed them, *otherwise* we'd have burnt down the village. The next time we will make an example."

We emphasize the word "*otherwise*" expressly, because it seems to show that in the early days of their appearance the *Franc-tireurs*, though not acknowledged as soldiers, were by some at all events admitted to have a sort of right to kill, which was denied to villagers. It was different afterwards, when bloodshed and retaliation so disgracefully embittered the war. To our question of whether the French officials and villagers were not as a rule courteous and civil to them? the answer was, "Oh, when we're in bodies, currishly civil (*houndisch freunidlich*), but when alone, they murder us like dogs."

After our coffee, we visited the battery of French twelve-pounders, and then left for Eix, the headquarters of the force round Verdun, bearing with us a note from one of the Bras officers to an *aide-de-camp* on the Staff of General Von Bothmer, who commanded at that point, and with the hope that we might have the opportunity of seeing from thence some shots exchanged with the fortress next day.

As a lesson in outpost duty, our visit in the morning to the pickets and sentries thrown out from Bras had been we felt more practically useful and instructive than many mornings' play at the same branch of a soldier's education in a peaceful garrison or camp.

It was not that we saw much that required any particular explanation or that was strikingly new to us.

As in the English service, the German advanced sentries are invariably (this they lay great stress on) posted double, never single, and the system carried out here of the furnishing and relief of the sentries by the *Feld-wach* or picket seemed to correspond substantially with our own. One or two minor points of departure from our strict peace regulations as laid down in the red book were to be noticed; for instance, every sentry was allowed to smoke, without any restriction, while on duty. Tobacco, in fact, is regarded as a stimulant to watchfulness, not as a somnolent, and a pipe is as universally cherished a portion of the German soldier's equipment as the weapon he carries, the Uhlans very generally having a long China one with a huge bowl suspended from the breast of their tunics.

But though in the system itself we saw no great divergence from our own, there was an earnestness in carrying it out, which naturally is not to be met with, or capable of being aroused, upon the drill field, or during a sham fight in peace.

The stooping gait of the patrols as, with their rifles ready at the thigh, they reconnoitred to the front through the close vineyards and wooded grounds; the care with which the spiked helmet was taken off, or the steel scabbard moved out of the way, so that there might be no tell-tale gleam from the rays of the sun: the well concealed spots chosen for the fires at which the pickets cooked; and many other small but interesting points, gave a sense of reality to what was going on. and therefore left an impression all the more clear and lasting.

The German troops at Bras consisted for the most part of *Landwehr*, and reserve, with an intermixture of the line. This mingling of the troops of different lengths of service we found to hold very generally (the *Landwehr* predominating) at the various points between Sedan and the neighbourhood of Metz; some of the officers—and, I think, almost invariably the senior ones—being officers *en permanence, i.e.,* regular officers.

The Englishman, from association of ideas, very often considers—and in spite of all one has read of the Prussian organization, (which will now be the model for all Germany,) until one actually sees the men themselves it is difficult to avoid doing so—that the *Landwehr* and reserve must be a less practised body of men than the line, in fact men corresponding to his own Militia and reserve forces in comparison with his own line.

Nothing could be wider from the fact than this idea, every Prussian having necessarily to serve three years (beginning at the age of twenty) with the colours, and then four with the *Landwehr*.

The *Landwehr*, man or officer, is merely one in the prime of life who has gone through his full three years' regular training, and some intermittent soldiering With the *Landwehr* as well; and as the wars with Denmark and Austria (in 1864 and 1866) have been so recently fought, a great proportion of the men we saw had served a campaign, and were decorated with one, two, and sometimes more medals.

The fact of the German army, by reason of the late wars, being so exceptionally trained just now (*Landwehr* and all) for active service, has not, we think, been generally sufficiently considered.

The nation is not only a nation of soldiers, by reason of every man having to serve and go through drill, but exceptionally just now a nation of campaigners.

With regard to the stamp of the *Landwehr* and reserve officers (to use a term which is expressive in England), it is only natural that, under a system which obliges all classes to serve in some capacity, the officer's rank will be sought for and obtained as a rule by men of comparatively good position, or of some kind of influence.

It results from this, that as the number of officers required is large, the upper and upper middle classes appear to furnish them. For instance, of those we met around Verdun, one was a nobleman of property; another a gentleman farmer, who meant, at the conclusion of the war, to go to Edinburgh to learn to manage his farm: a third was putting in his time in the college which qualifies in Germany for the Department of Woods and Forests, and hoping to find, eventually, (as others have done, and as some of our officers do) employment in that department under the British government in India: a fourth was a mining engineer; a fifth a man of means, who had left London suddenly to return to Germany and do his duty with his regiment.

As a class, in fact, they correspond very nearly to that which officers the English army.

All of the officers above alluded to, though called away at the outbreak of the war from civilian employment of all kinds, (and not ashamed to admit that they longed for peace), looked perfectly at home as soldiers, into which career they had been fully initiated, and all had the manner of gentlemen.

In Prussia they do not approve of any but gentlemen holding commissions, and it was evident that, whether from prejudice or not, the officers had been strengthened in their views by their experience of the French officers and the discipline of their army in this war.

As the whole nation, however, must serve, it follows that there are many gentlemen unable to obtain commissions, and who must enter the ranks, and it results from this, and from the general education of the country, that the status of the rank and file is raised, and that the officers have a greater *entente cordiale* with their men than would otherwise be the case.

They showed them, I could see, in a marked manner, every possible respect and thoughtfulness, while keeping up at the same time a strict discipline.

When an educated rank and file under a trained caste of officers, united in feeling and with a large; amount of European field experience, is handled and looked after by men of exceptional talent for administration and strategy, no wonder that under a Von Roon and a Möltke it has succeeded as it has.

There is a satisfaction in thinking that in many respects the English army bears a strong resemblance to the German, and that when trained and handled, and above all administered as well, it will accomplish as much—to say *more*, in view of what has been done in this war, would be meaningless. In minor details of dress and equipment, we have, I suspect, little to learn from either cavalry or infantry, nor do I think from artillery.

In speaking as above of the German army, I speak of both officers and men as a class. Exceptions are to be found to all rules, and we met with one or two very ordinary specimens of the German officer and with many slovenly louts of soldiers, but they were exceptions and were not rules.

It was past five when we left Bras, and became dusk while we were still upon the road leading round by the North of Verdun to Eix.

To be out after sunset was, we found, under our circumstances a decided mistake. In the first place we lost the way, though only for a time, and the sensation of doing this at night in an unquiet district is not agreeable; in the next place we had a small difficulty with one of the German posts, which was aggravated, if not caused, by our being abroad at so late an hour.

At every village we had passed through after leaving Bras we had been asked for our papers by the examining party of a non-commissioned officer and three or four men at the entrance; but about dusk we reached the village of Fleury, and not being stopped, passed on towards the centre of the place, expecting there to have to show our papers, when we were suddenly and very sharply ordered to halt and descend, and were brought by some soldiers before an officer, whom we saw was in a towering passion.

He asked us what we meant by avoiding his sentries and entering the village, and who we were? and to our reply that no sentries had challenged us on the road, and that we were travellers taking an interest in his profession, and who wanted to see the war, he answered by sending in great indignation for the sentries, who were soon confronted with us, telling us at the same time in French that travelling at nightfall through the outposts of any army for the "pleasure of seeing war" was hardly, in his opinion, a likely story, that no *soldiers*, as we said we were, would attempt to pass a sentry; and that, at all events, we'd better stay till the following morning in his guard-room, when he'd escort us out to see some more French shells (*obus*) than he thought we'd care about.

All this time he was too angry to pay much attention to our passports, &c, which we kept trying to show to him, and his ill-temper was still further increased by a sergeant, who whispered to him in German, "Lieutenant, you forget that you are speaking in French; the people here (by that time a small crowd of curious villagers had collected near us) have heard you mention the intention to open fire in the morning."

"Who are your sympathies with?" he now said, turning to us, (rather a narrow-minded remark, by the way,) and on our replying, "With you, and also with the French; we are English, as we tell you, and are neutrals;" he gave a sort of "Humph," as much as to imply that that was a description of animal for whom he had the most unmitigated and peculiar contempt.

Altogether, when at last the two sentries came up and grounded their rifles upon each side of us, we made up our minds to an uncomfortable night of it.

I shall always think that it was most creditable to the character of the German soldier that these sentries, when very angrily questioned by their officer, told the exact truth, admitting they had seen, but not stopped us. They urged some misunderstanding of their orders, and were at length severely reprimanded and dismissed. It would have been easy for them to have endeavoured to screen themselves at our expense.

This admission of the sentries mollified our friend's disposition towards us, and on a careful perusal of our passports, and especially of the letter we bore with us from the officer at Bras, he made every apology for his hastiness and passed us on to Eix.

The inconvenience we suffered was not very great, but it is unpleasant to have one's assertions roughly questioned; and any traveller arriving so late with a mere passport (or without any private letter), especially if weak in languages, would probably have passed the night in the guard-room.

When we arrived at Eix we reported ourselves at General Von Bothmer's headquarters, and found him and his Staff at a late dinner, and upon sending in our passports and letter, were received with great kindness, being at once asked by the general to join them at table and offered a bed by the officer (Graf Von Kospoth), to whose good offices we had been recommended, and who was billeted in the house of a French villager a little way off.

It was arranged to mount us the following morning, that we might see the bombardment of Verdun (the first that took place), which was to begin at 6 a.m., from the different French batteries around the town, and of which we had received some inkling before leaving Bras.

As it happened that the general, some of his officers and ourselves had mutual acquaintances in Hanover, this meeting was all the more pleasant for us, and after an enjoyable two hours we turned in, feeling that we were very lucky to be in our present quarters, instead of in the guard-room, which had once threatened us so imminently at Fleury.

The next morning we were up before daylight, and after a cup of coffee rode with the general and his Staff to another portion of the same heights of Belleville we had been on at Bras, and stopped at Belleville, about two-and-a half miles off, passing on the road one of the field batteries on its way to take up its position.

A "Good morning," called out by one of the officers to the men of the battery, was responded to by a very cheery and universal "*Morgen, Morgen*" from the latter, a sort of interchange between the different ranks upon the line of march, which sounded strangely to an English ear, but very well and hearty, notwithstanding. Arrived at our destination, we rode with Graf Von Kospoth, who remained with us through the morning, to a point from whence we could see Verdun lying beneath us at Bras, but at a greater distance off, and where we stayed waiting till the puffs of smoke should rise from the crests behind which were the German batteries. At length they curled upwards from some three different points into the air, and the bombardment began.

As we have before, mentioned, the German guns were of small calibre, and the object of the day's firing was not so much to do any great damage to the works, which could hardly be hoped for, as to show the besieged that they were now surrounded, and thus deter them from further sorties; to try and drive the signalmen from the cathedral towers, and to test the range and power of the captured French battery. To fire upon a cathedral is generally considered an act of vandalism in war; but, at the same time, it is clear that if its towers are used openly as advantageous positions for signalmen, the general who respects them will be charged, and justly so, by his own soldiers as having more regard for the preservation of buildings than of their lives. In fact, if they are to be viewed as sacred, they ought not to be made use of as a means of actively annoying the besiegers. The German officers expressed regret, which, from their manner, I believe was sincerely felt, at having to direct their shot against the tower, and it is only fair that those (as we ourselves have often done), who exclaim loudly against tiring at cathedrals, should hear the German side of the question.

For some twenty minutes there was no response from the fortress to the German challenge—the garrison, which had hitherto been left pretty well to itself, being evidently unprepared for so early an attack upon it. At length, however, the citadel, one of the bastions and a ravelin began to reply, and from that time the firing went on steadily from both sides for some three-and-a-half hours, whom General Von Bothmer ordered the German batteries to cease. There is something, after all, partaking of the monotonous in a bombardment. The little clouds of smoke, the booming reports, and the rattling of the shells as they burst in the streets, are repeated again and again, and though exciting at first, the interest ceases before long, and we were; not sorry when at length the French were left in peace.

The result of the morning had been to prove that though the field batteries could not to any useful extent oppose the heavier artillery of the works, the French ammunition and guns could be handled with good effect. Twice the town appeared to have been set on fire, but the flames were on both occasions speedily got under. The loss on the German side was very slight, being only one *sous*-officer killed, and some four men and an officer wounded. Of the French loss, of course, we were ignorant. It was stated to be the intention to wait until the arrival of heavy guns from Toul, which had just fallen, before renewing the bombardment.[2]

During the bombardment we rode to many different points, visiting, as at Bras, some of the advanced pickets and sentries, and seeing much that was of interest.

The accuracy of the French artillery fire, and the fact of their firing at any chance horsemen (as asserted at Bras) was clearly proved to us; for at one time our companion, having previously sent forward some men to clear a neighbouring vineyard from any chance *Franc-tireur*,

---

2. Subsequently a continuous fire from the heavy guns caused the surrender of the place by Baron Guerin de Waldersbach, the Governor, without awaiting an assault.

had taken us up to within about 1,700 yards of the outworks, where we were having an excellent view, as we hoped, unobserved. To our serious disappointment we found we had been perceived, a cloud of smoke came out of a hitherto silent embrasure directly in our front, and as we saw it and galloped off, a well-aimed shell pitched and burst within ten yards of where we had just been standing, but luckily a little beyond, so that its pieces did us no damage.

I think few people would care to enjoy a view under these circumstances. None of us did, but we rapidly changed ground, being; rewarded for so doing by a second shell, which, aimed more hurriedly than the first, went without bursting, well over our heads, our companion muttering contemptuously—"Time!" meaning that the shell was, he believed, fired with a time fuse, of the efficacy of which fuses, as compared with their own percussion, all the German officers we met with were in the habit, rightly or wrongly, of expressing a poor opinion. They consider that at present no time fuse (our own included) has been invented which is sufficiently simple, and at the same time can be made to explode the shell with such accuracy as to render it as good all round as their own permission.

As we disappeared down a valley, round the corner of a little brick cattle shed, our companion called out to a picket near it to "Take care," as the French would probably think we had entered it, and the truth of his supposition was proved by our seeing, a few moments afterwards, two shells in succession burst almost on the walls of the building.

We were at this time standing with two or three other officers in a small mustard field, and the practice of the enemy seemed to strike them. "We had better move from here," one of them said, "and separate a little; the French are firing too well, and dark uniforms are conspicuous on the yellow ground."

The time fuses did their work well, at all events on this occasion, though, from the warning given, they fortunately caused no loss, and we gave the Verdun batteries a wider berth for the remainder of the morning.

After returning to Eix, and while the general and his Staff were at the business of the day, we amused ourselves in walking about the grounds of the small French *chateau* in which we were quartered, and, to while away the time, sat down by the side of a fishpond full of carp, which came swimming up to us to be fed, and wrote up our notebooks, which for two or three days had been allowed to fall behindhand. The owners of this *chateau* had evidently been fond of field

165

sports, for there was a kennel on the grounds containing several dogs, all with more or less of the fox-hound and pointer breed in them—one, according to a French servant's assertion (though we must withhold our corroboration) being pure English. "Ah!" he said, as they pawed the bars and were clamorous to get out, "*Ils n' iront pas à la chasse cette année!*"

What a change the war had caused in the surroundings and brought to the owners of this bright-looking country house!

Outside the flower-beds were trampled down and neglected, the walks unswept, the lawn strewn with leaves and rubbish; while inside the enemy clanked about the passages, and lounged on the sofas, and spread his maps upon the table, planning the conquest of the French garrison not four miles distant, of which, perhaps, the owner of this very property formed a part.

About one o'clock we had luncheon with the general and his Staff—the mayor, nominally in honour of our visit, but a good deal, we imagine, to conciliate the Prussians, coming in person to look after us, and sending in his best wine, *curaçoa*, cigars, and all kinds of luxuries. I am ashamed to say we did full justice to them; I say *ashamed*, for we did not like him or his civility (the excess of which could have pleased no one) in our hearts. These officials had undoubtedly a hard game to play; but making all due allowance for that, we can quite understand why the French Emperor dismissed one of them early in the war for attention to the Germans, which he; considered amounted to want of patriotism.

The general very kindly offered to forward us on the next stage to Etain in his carriage, a large sort of covered waggonette, the property in peaceful times of the mayor, but now at his temporary disposal. While we were at luncheon, a lieutenant of *Cuirassiers* came in from Etain a make a report to his chief, the purport of which will serve to show with what weak detachments some of the links of the chain of communication between Verdun and Metz were held.

It was (he told us himself afterwards) that in consequence of some changes he felt so dangerously weak, that he considered it his duty to ask the general for a reinforcement. He had only twelve troopers in a town of several hundred people, (and no other soldiers in it), "Jolly little," he said, "to keep them in order." Yet he put a bold face upon it, and on the general, for reasons best known to himself, refusing more men, appeared to dismiss the matter once for all from his mind.

Such a weak party would seem almost to have courted murder;

but, of course, it was well understood in Etain what the fate of the village and inhabitants would have been, had it been attempted.

In a discussion at the table today, it was said that the French *chassepot* carried so much further than the needle-gun, that the Germans often had to march some 800 yards under its fire before they could return a shot, and that their men began to drop from it at a distance of 1800 yards; that the French fought very bravely at various times, but that they came into action, firing away without taking aim, (often without bringing their rifles to the shoulder,) in the most reckless manner, and when once repulsed would not come again with any determination to the attack. Their own men (*i.e.,* the Germans) had the habit, it was said, of always giving three; distinct hurrahs! one after the other, just before going into a fight.

At about three o'clock, we said goodbye to our hosts at Eix, whose kind welcome of us we shall never forget, and as we set off in the carriage drawn by four horses for Etain, and accompanied along the road by the lieutenant of *Cuirassiers*, who was riding back to his post, we could not help surmising what particular description of *grandee* the peasants, who doffed their caps to us along the road, most probably took us for; whether, being in plain clothes, only for Bismarck and his secretary, or for two greater autocrats in disguise. We say "greater autocrats," because in military-ridden Germany we have heard even Bismarck himself (simply because he has for years been in civil employ) spoken of in a tone of half disparagement as only "a mere civilian."

CHAPTER 6

Verdun to Metz, by Gravelotte

At Etain the *Cuirassier* officer got us a waggon and horse through the mayor, and after spending half-an-hour with him in his comfortable quarters in the Mairie—the most luxurious we had seen—we pushed on towards Conflans, which we reached just before dusk. Our drive; of this afternoon was not a very cheerful one. The country had a melancholy, deserted look, and the poor old driver was evidently dismally frightened by our having impressed him.

"Oh," he; said, "when a man goes away now, one never knows when he will come back. Do, *Messieurs*, give me a paper, so that no one will take me after I get to Conflans. When *Monsieur le Maire* impressed me, my wife and three children all began to cry; there is no tilling or sowing going on while I'm away, and they thought I might never return."

We told him he need not be afraid of us, and that he would be sent back that very night with a "*sauf conduit*" without fail; but we said, "You must expect evils in time of war; why did you wish for war?"

"Ah, *Monsieur*, I never wished for war; we only lose by war; that was that miserable Emperor."

"Yes," we replied, "but you voted for the Emperor; everybody knew that that meant voting for war? Didn't you vote for the Empire in the Plebiscite?"

"Plebiscite, *Monsieur*, what's the plebiscite? I don't understand you, *Monsieur*." Apparently he had never even heard of it!

Presently an old man came up to us on the road, thinking probably we might have some authority to interfere, and wringing his hands. "*Monsieur, ils prennant toutes le vaches*," (they are taking all my cows,) pointing to a field where we could see some German soldiers driving off the animals before them. Of course, we could do nothing to help him; but his distress did not tend to raise our spirits.

Arrived at Conflans, we met once more with a very good reception from the captain in command of the company (260 men) forming the garrison, who asked us to join him and his officers at their dinner in one of the little *auberges* of the village.

The inhabitants of Conflans bore the look of having been greatly oppressed and ground down by the war; there was a miserable dejected air about them, and we felt that we were nearing the circle where the requisitions of the large army around Metz were telling heavily.

From the window of the *auberge* the ambulance flag still hung out, and a wounded French officer occupied the next room to us, an unmistakeable hospital odour pervading the whole house.

We felt as if, being non-combatants, we were unjustifiably where we were, as we evidently, though unintentionally, inconvenienced others.

The landlady of the *auberge*, a wretched and overworked little woman, on the commandant telling her to find us a room, became very loud in her remonstrances. She had, she said, but three rooms (not counting the wounded officer's) in which she could put us. In one, all the officers dined, and afterwards a sick son and his attendant slept. In another, she and her family lived, and in the third (the kitchen) some soldiers had just been billeted. The commandant first looked about to see with his own eyes if it were true, and then insisted upon changing the soldiers' billet, and the family moving downstairs gave us up their room.

Four subaltern officers, the captain, and an assistant-surgeon, sat down to dinner with us. One of the subalterns had just come from a University and was dubbed "Professor" by the rest,—a nickname which amused us, as it is so common a one, applied for much the same reasons in our own service, "The Professor will tell you," was generally the reply of one of the others when some question was put which he felt himself unable to answer, and from the Professor and others we gained a good deal of information about the German soldiers and the war.

The pay of the infantry privates in their army left them, they told us, (after all deductions,) about threepence or fourpence a day. They had but one regular meal each day, and nothing but water allowed as a drink—we mean by this, allowed by the State—and they carried a weight upon the march of about sixty pounds.

With regard to the impossibility which it was formerly the fashion

to prophesy, of restraining men when using breech-loaders from firing away too rapidly all their ammunition, they said that they could
completely control this, and that in practice it had not been found
any drawback to the breech-loader. Evidently the detachment there
was looking ahead to the prospect of having to hut itself in the cold
weather, for they were already taking the windows and sashes out of
all the abandoned French houses, with the view of using them for
huts. They did not, however, it was told us, despoil in this way any
buildings whose owners had remained in them, but anything in a deserted house they took, if they wanted it.

The telegraph wires it had been found at first difficult to preserve,
but, after two or three peasants had been hung, they were left unmo-
lested.

Our night at Conflans cannot be described as a very pleasant one,
for our quarters were the complete reverse of inviting, but we slept
soundly nevertheless, and the following morning took a stroll through
the village with Capt. B———. Two or three of the villagers surrounded
him at once, with complaints such as that wheat had been taken from
them for some horses, and so on, and to all these he listened patiently
enough, though for most of them he could offer but little redress,
"The horses must be fed," he said, "and if oats are not provided. why
I must take wheat."

With what a torrent of shrill sound a French, woman, when ex-
cited, can pour out her words; and though we sincerely pitied the
people of this and all the other French villages suffering from the war,
we felt some little sympathy with Capt. B———, when, after listening for three or four minutes, he said to one of these, in had French,
"*Parlez lentenuint, Badame. Je no comprends un mot, Badame; vouz parlez
comme un moulin à vent.*"

In passing the market place, we saw printed in conspicuous char-
acters that "Anybody found carrying arms, who did not belong to
regularly organized corps, should be shot,"—a notice aimed, of course
at the *Franc-tireurs*, who were now becoming a great thorn in the side
of the Prussians. After our stroll we turned our attention to the question of how we should get on towards Metz, and in our endeavour,
assisted by Capt. B———, to settle it by obtaining a conveyance, we
were present at a scene which would have amused us, if we had been
able to look at the thing only in its ludicrous light.

We may say here that it was always our custom when we obtained
waggons to pay for them at liberal rates, and to obtain for them a per-

170

mit from the German authorities to return at once; but the peasants had been so long unaccustomed to receive money in return for their services, and had so often been pressed away for days together, that it was not very easy to persuade them before starting that they would be paid, or in reality sent back. For these reasons it was occasionally difficult to procure conveyances, even with the aid of the commandant, the peasants trying to dodge the requisitions as far as they possibly dare.

At Conflans this was the case; the mayor, on being sent for, affirmed positively that there was no conveyance, and that it was impossible to get one. He was told, "*Mais, Monsieur le Maire. il n'y a pas d' impossible. Il le faut,*" and while he was gently invited to try in one direction, the commandant walked with us to try in another. Still it was in vain at first that we sought for a waggon; everything that was ferreted out had something smashed about it and was not available. At last, a tall sergeant came up and whispered with a grin that he had seen a good light trap the evening before in the garden of a house close by, and volunteered to guide us to it. The trap was found, but the wheels were all gone, hidden, the sergeant said, by the sly owners. "*Sie sind so schlan,*" (They are so sly,) was his indignant exclamation.

The owner contended, with an odd sort of logic, that as one of the wheels had been broken, he had been obliged to send all for repair; but on being cross-examined as to this assertion, he became confused in his statements. A short examination of the premises now took place, but failed to produce the wheels, and we were beginning to wonder whether we should have to interfere, and try and save the waggoner from the German anger, and also when our own waggon troubles were to end, when a find elsewhere was reported. Away we went to look at it, and springless and bad as it was, we voted it a treasure. An old grey horse was harnessed to it by all sorts of extraordinary straps and strings, a thin rope was made to do duty for reins, and then an ancient-looking, toothless peasant clambered up, and we were ready to start. The commandant had proposed sending a soldier with us, but as it was a matter of impossibility to squeeze more than three into the vehicle, we set off without him, feeling that one man could hardly be much protection to us in case of meeting any chance *Franc-tireur*—the possible bogie whom we had to dread.

Our journey at first was a very slow one. Hitherto our animals had all been too tired to be troublesome, but this beast was an exception, and carried us by a sudden dash so nearly over the edge of a steep precipice, that we both jumped out, fortunately lighting on our feet. To make a long story short, we were much relieved when, with hands cut by the rope reins (for we took to driving ourselves), we reached Gravelotte, *via* Doncourt, having had many anxious moments on the road, and shaves of going over embankments, and into poplar trees and German detachments; for as we continued on our route we were passed at frequent intervals by parties of infantry and cavalry, the latter generally escorting supplies.

While approaching Gravelotte our attention was attracted by a group of German soldiers staring and pointing towards, and following the direction of their gaze we saw a balloon high in air, evidently just come out of Metz, now about twelve miles distant, and sailing along under a fair wind towards Paris. It was far out of shot, so that no attempt was made to molest it.

Arrived at Gravelotte itself, which is only about four miles from the fort of Mont St. Quentin, and the French outposts around Metz, the number of troops that we met increased. Rifles were piled and guns parked near the village, and cavalry troopers in twos and threes moved over the fields to the left of the road, clearly links in the chain which Prince Frederick Charles had drawn around Marshal Bazaine and his army, cooped up in their stronghold.

Not very far from the entrance of the village, and to the left hand, the blackened walls of what was once the farmhouse of Malmaison, bore evidence to the effect of the French shells which were poured into it, and its garden, held by the Germans, on the morning of the 18th of August.

We had no time to give more than a short two hours to the field of Gravelotte, for it was necessary for us to reach Corny, some miles off, by a country road, which was sure to be blocked up pretty well by German convoys, and to find our quarters there before nightfall. Still, in that two hours, we saw a great deal of the scene of the struggle at and around the village. First of all we bent our steps eastward along the Metz road, to the point where it crosses the ravine running between the Bois des Ognons and Bois de Vaux towards Ais, the further bank of which was the scene of the desperate assault of the Germans against the French left, protected by *Mitrailleurs* placed behind entrenchments, tier above tier, upon the slope.

Passing along this road, raised high over the ravine, the German cavalry was mown down as it endeavoured to charge across it and reach the French position on the other side. One can imagine the attempt in war of a much more desperate nature than the advance of infantry and cavalry over such a ground (the cavalry necessarily confined to the road itself) against an enemy's batteries massed on the opposing wooded heights; and that the Germans were successful here and at other spots, such as Spichheren, would, if no other proof were forthcoming, stamp them as soldiers as daring and excellent in attack as troops can well be.

Returning through Gravelotte we walked over the plateau which lies to the south of the village between the Rezonville road and the thick woods of the Bois des Ognons and Bois de Vaux. Across this plateau, now worn completely bare of grass or cultivation, the columns of the 1st Army Corps moved to the attack of Gravelotte and the position beyond. An eye-witness of the battle describes the Bois des Ognons as appearing on the afternoon of the 18th to hold all Germany, and the dark German columns as winding out of it like huge snakes, which were cut in pieces by the French *Mitrailleurs*, but, always joining together again, glided ever onwards towards Gravelotte and the ravine beyond.

Fragments of shells, bullets, remnants of accoutrements, and mounds of earth surmounted by the rough wooden cross, marked the spots where many had fought and fallen in the fight; and near the northwest corner of the Bois des Ognons,—just where the ground slopes sharply down to a valley and a country road winds up close to the trees,—the little heaps of *Mitrailleur* cartridge holders showed the position of a French battery, the spot being one from which a clear range could be had towards Rezonville.

From this point we struck into the Rezonville Road, and returned by it to Gravelotte. All along this road the tall poplar trees had been cut down at intervals (usually every alternate tree) to give range to the French guns. The houses of the village on the side towards Rezonville were loop-holed, and so were the stone walls enclosing the gardens and fields, but, as at Bazeilles, no communication between houses to assist street fighting had been made. One of the walls on the south side of the village, and which flanked the plateau over which the Germans must have moved from the Bois des Ognons, afforded an interesting example of rough loop-holing.

It was not a high wall, perhaps less than five feet high, but was pierced with two tiers of loop-holes by simply knocking out the stones. The loop-holes of the lower tier were not directly under those of the upper, but one of them (speaking roughly) was placed underneath the centre of the space between two upper ones, thus,

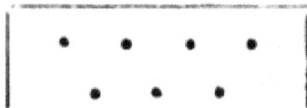

This seemed to us a good practical way of combining a large number of loop-holes with convenience of firing in a wall too low to admit of the stereotyped method of two tiers of loop-holes, one above the other, with a platform for the upper rank of men to stand on.

All the men firing could do so unseen, and the wall was not much weakened.

The troops passing over the plateau under musketry and *mitrailleur* fire ought to have found it (as it seemed to us) more difficult even than they did to carry the village and press on to the position beyond,

The village was comparatively little damaged by shells. The whole of the country around Gravelotte, with the exception of the sides of the deeply-wooded ravine where the French left rested, is of a gentle undulating character, passable, generally speaking, for all arms, but covered here and there with large belts of thickish wood. The French left resting as it did on the wooded hillside, might, we should imagine, have been made almost impregnable if the American system of felling the trees to form breastworks (although these trees are not so favourable for this as American fir trees,) had been resorted to.

Leaving Gravelotte between one and two o'clock, we drove down a winding and steep road along the densely-wooded valley of the Moselle to Ars. From Ars we drove to Noveant, where we crossed the Moselle, about eighty yards wide and with a dry bed, by a suspension bridge, and soon found ourselves in Corny, the headquarters of Prince Frederick Charles. The rich wooded scenery between Gravelotte and Corny is of peculiar beauty, and we should look forward with great pleasure to the prospect of seeing it again in times of peace. Today heavy clouds of dust, partially obscuring the view, hung in the air, raised by convoy after convoy of supplies, and by troop after troop of foot and horse, the incessant stream of which gave to us some faint idea of what the presence of such a vast body of soldiers really implied: and it was only after frequent halts, during which we choked patiently by the hot roadsides to let the columns pour on, that we reached our destination as the, day was drawing to a close.

There was apparently but little excitement in Corny that day, but yet Marshall Bazaine had made upon it one of his few efforts to disturb the German beleaguering army.

A sortie had been made on a point of the German circle some distance from Corny towards Peltre, Meray-le-Haut, and Colombey, which had been repulsed, the Germans burning these villages after they had defeated the enemy.

Perhaps nothing could give a better idea of the magnitude of the German lines than the fact that we were unaware of the sortie until the following morning, and as it was not mentioned by any one in conversation, we believe that (with the exception, of course, of those at headquarters,) no one at Corny was better informed about it than ourselves.

We soon found that to obtain quarters here would be a difficult matter indeed. Every corner of the place was occupied by soldiers, and in the general squeezing, crushing, and scarcity of all the comforts of life that prevailed, civility seemed to be at a discount; a cold "No," was all we could at first get to our request for a lodging, and after several efforts to obtain one, we at last thought ourselves in extreme luck, because we secured the free use of the floor of the tap room of a little *auberge*, absolutely swarming with flies, and where the field post of one of the army corps was established. We ought to say the free use of it after 10 p.m., for up to that hour the room was filled by soldiers, who sat drinking and talking with great quietness and order at the little tables, until the bugles summoned them to their billets. As for a room to ourselves, or a bed anywhere, such a thing was not to be had for money, and eatables were almost as unobtainable.

We managed to get a little chocolate and bread, but meat was not to be procured, and eggs, the landlady told us, were so scarce, that even those not over fresh sold for fourpence apiece.

To get a waggon, or any species of conveyance, or horse, would be, we were informed, an utter impossibility; so we came to an arrangement by which our driver was given an official permission to take us on a stage further next day, he himself unwillingly agreeing to it, as we had paid him already a fair sum, and the authority of the permit set his mind at rest.

How it must wear the heart out of a human being to have to toil from morning until night, as the poor landlady of this *auberge* had, for those who are at deadly strife with one's husband and children, and nearest and dearest friends. One of her sons, she told us, was shut up in Metz, whence the cannonading could be heard almost daily. Another was in Paris, and her husband was fighting in some third portion of

France.

Certainly this poor soul was given little time to think over her woes, for there was no rest in Corny for the *auberge* keepers, and, perhaps, all the happier for them.

During the evening we wandered up to the billet of one of the officers of the headquarter staff, to whom our hosts at Eix had given us a letter, asking him to get permission for us to travel by the railway from Courcelles towards Saarbrück. This we obtained, as well as fresh instructions as to how we could best see Metz the following morning; and then after a stroll through the village streets, and past the large white *chateau* where the band of the Guards was playing opposite Prince Frederick Charles' headquarters, we went back again to the *auberge*, and sat listening to the conversation of the soldiers as they talked and smoked at the tables.

There was no noisy argument among these soldiers, still less any pot-house wrangling or drunkenness through the evening. In fact, from all we saw of the German private soldiers on this trip, we should put them down us being generally a very well-behaved set of men, though we do not doubt that many isolated instances of brutality and crime may be brought against them.

After they had gone out the landlady brought up a mattress to place on the floor, and having opened the windows, to let in the fresh air and to let out the close smoky atmosphere, we lay down for the night, our driver luxuriously occupying the top of a billiard table in the same apartment.

The next morning, after a rather uncomfortable night of it, we were up betimes, and at 6 a. m. were climbing the hill of St. Blaise, from which we knew that Metz could be distinctly seen. That disappointment so often experienced by those who look forward to mountain views was in store for us now. When we readied the summit we could see no further than a few hundred yards. A field battery of twelve pounders placed behind a stone wall, covered over and heightened with earth, and revetted with fascines, lay close at our feet in readiness to repel sorties.

On our right was a small sort of farmhouse, with an enclosure, admission to which, by a recent order posted up on the wall, was stringently forbidden to all but the Headquarters Staff, for whose use a large telescope had been erected within its precincts. To our left stood an old ruined tower, but below a dense fog hung in the air, obscuring everything from view. Some German artillerymen, seeing we were strangers, entered into conversation; With us, and told us that the mist did not rise generally before 10 a. m., so that down we went again to Corny, and after having breakfasted returned once more to the hill. If we had suffered some little disappointment on our earlier journey, we were at all events repaid for it by the glorious panorama which burst upon us on our second visit.

Metz, with its cathedral spires glittering in the morning sun, lay beneath us, and the River Moselle could be traced in many points of its course as it wound round and through the town. Fort St. Quentin stood out prominently towards our left front; to our right rose the smoke of the burning woods and villages of Colombey, Peltre and Mercy le Haut, which had been the scenes of the sortie of the day before. The many dips and hollows visible from the height were filled with the dark-coated German troops as far as the eye could reach, and with a glass at one point some advanced sentries of both French and Germans could he seen running quickly from fence to fence, and then crouching down, apparently skirmishing with one another, while away from the other side of Metz the deadened reports of the guns of St. Julien struck at intervals upon the ear.

We have said that at Corny the people seemingly knew absolutely nothing of the last sortie, but now one of the artillerymen on the hill pointed us out the burning villages, saying that there had been fighting there on the previous day, and drew our attention also to the French and German sentries we have described, who were, it seems, stalking each other for the "fun (as he explained it to us with a laugh) of obtaining a shot."

Since we gazed upon these rising columns of smoke and watched these sentinels, two books have been published, from which we hope we may be forgiven for quoting extracts. One is called *The Fall of Metz*, by Mr. G. T. Robinson, an Englishman shut up in the town throughout the siege; the other, *What I saw of the War*, by the Hon. C. Allanson Winn.

Until we read these extracts we had no idea of the very ruthless nature of the struggle for the villages, whose smoking ruins we saw, and within three miles of which we passed that afternoon, or of the tiger-like thirst for blood which by degrees had taken hold of both armies. We doubt if in any of the wars of previous times more savage things in the way of fire and sword have been enacted than have taken place in this one, and (from these extracts seemingly) around Metz.

Mr. Robinson says, that on the 27th September (the day we ar-

177

rived at Corny) it was determined to make a reconnaissance in force from Metz towards Peltre, Colombey, Mercy le Haut, and other points, and to endeavour during it to destroy a German depot of provisions at the Peltre railway station, and bring in what cattle, grain, &c., could be got there to Metz.

This sortie was so far successful that the railway station at Peltre was reached, the provisions secured, and the German outposts driven in.

Mr. Robinson, who was a spectator of some portion of the fighting, thus describes it:—

Meanwhile another portion of our force pushes on rapidly to the village (Peltre), where, before the Prussians have recovered from their surprise, we, are on them. They run to a convent— the convent of the Sisters of Providence it was called,—its walls are already loop-holed; but under a deadly fire an entrance is forced, and now commences a horrible sight for those poor, peace-loving sisters. Their church was turned into a charnel-house, their very sanctuary was stained with blood, and the house of mercy became the house of vengeance, for there was no mercy there. *The Prussians craved, the French gave no quarter,* and flight there was none.

A similarly bloody and yet more barbarous scene is described as being carried on simultaneously at Mercy le Haut.

The Prussians have since our last visit turned it into a fortress. The windows are boarded up and loop-holed, and they have constructed an abattis of trees in front of the *chateau.* They are soon driven out of the first line of fallen trees, and then comes the attack upon the house itself. Doors are smashed in, the wooden protection of the window's cut to pieces, and, with a shout of '*Vive la France!*' at them rushed the soldiers. It is vengeance now, the quick blood of the Frenchman is on fire, and the dogged resistance of the Teuton rendered more determined than before. Each room on the ground floor is a slaughterhouse, and as it is impossible to ascend the staircase, and the garrison won't yield, the infuriated soldiers heap up everything inflammable *and set fire to it.*

Good God! it is horrible to think what demons war makes men. Every despairing face that appears at the upper windows is shot at before the man who owns it has time to cry for quarter. The flames and the smoke mount upwards, higher and higher ascends the smoke, higher and higher leap the flames, taking death with them, and that that death may be a speedy one is the only mercy to be hoped for now at Mercy le Haut." And now all around us rise huge columns of smoke in the air, for the enemy is determined to burn up what we have left. The whole village of Peltre is in a blaze; the long forks of flame start up into dense smoke clouds, which roll over the valley, and all that day and all that night does it blaze away.

The Grange-aux-Bois is yet in flames, the wood and *chateau* of Colombey are burning, and as we retire the Prussians advance and burn La Maxe.

From this date until the Marshal began to treat definitely for the capitulation of the place, scarcely a day passed but that the investing forces set fire to some farm or some village, and the horizon was black by day and red by night from the smoke and fire of these barbarous incendiaries.

The shooting down of sentries and *videttes*, with no especial object—that is, with no further military aim than that of killing the individual soldier—seems to have been thought an honourable exhibition of prowess by both sides.

In describing a street in Metz with its motley crowd of occupants, Mr. Robinson thus draws the picture of a French sentry-slayer, whose achievements we may privately doubt, but who was at all events held in great respect as a hero:—

Now occurs a gap, and from out of the midst of all this colour stepped a short, thick-set man. All raised their hats to him, many stepped up to him and exchanged a hurried word or two as he walked rapidly along with his swinging step. That was Hitter. His name almost tempts a pun. He achieved a reputation here by going out in front of the '*avant postes*' and bringing down the Prussian *videttes* and sentries. This morning he shook his head rather mournfully. He had only killed six during the night, and thought that a poor night's work. Good heavens! we *smile* at his discomfiture, so hardened does war make us. Six empty homes and six dead men were nothing to us then; and it was more with a pondering mind as to whether it is right to shoot down sentinels and '*avant postes*' than with a horror at their death that I turned away. Murder and war seem too nearly allied here to be honourable.

Now for the Prussian proceedings, as told by the Hon. C. Allanson Winn:—

Von Schmeling was most anxious to see the Vaux outposts (one of the outposts close to Metz). About 900 yards off was a little chapel situated in the corner of a vineyard sloping down the hill from Jussy. In this chapel two French soldiers were situated on fore-post duty. Presently we saw one of them walk quietly down through the vineyard to a tree which stood exactly in the middle of it. Returning to the picket, we suggested away through the vines by which a couple of Prussians might easily get within shot of him when he tried to return to the chapel, Two men at once set out, and we soon lost sight of them in the bright green foliage. We now returned to the Scotch fir to *watch the development of the plot.*

We won't continue this story beyond saying that the Frenchman, having quietly picked a few apples off the tree, was on the point of returning, when two needle-gun bullets whizzed close past him, but missed, and that he then very wisely got behind the tree again, when these observers of the development of the plot retired, "feeling sure that the two Prussians would watch him until night, if necessary."

To most minds the killing of sentries (unless it is absolutely necessary, as a preliminary to some contemplated military operation, to get rid of them, when it is, of course, justifiable to surprise and kill them if they resist,) must seem, if not absolute murder, at all events exceedingly unchivalrous. No object of importance can be gained by it, and this has been very generally recognized in other wars.

One seems to have gone back during the last half-century, when one contrasts with the above the accounts given in Napier's *History of the Peninsula War* of the friendly way in which the outposts of the English and French armies fraternized in Spain, and also the stories of the good feeling with which interchanges of chaff, such as, "How are you, Yank?" and so on, occasionally went on between the troops of the North and South in the late War of Secession,

As we were upon the hill of St. Blaise a company of Poles from Prussian Poland marched up, and struck us very much by their fine figures and martial bearing, generally, they had the very fair hair and light blue eyes which form the type of the Saxon race, and were above the ordinary height. This was the finest body of men we noticed in our travels, although the Germans, as a rule, are strong and large men.

About half-past eleven we went down the hill once more towards Corny, passing by many small vineyards, where the grapes were rotting upon the vines for want of hands to gather them, and were nearly at the foot, when cannon shot after cannon shot from a distance, and a long sort of cheer coming upon the air from the direction of Metz, sent us half-way up again for the third time.

Before we reached the summit, though, all firing had ceased; the sentry was pacing carelessly on his former beat. We could see the soldiers lounging about, evidently looking at nothing in particular, and so putting this temporary excitement down to a few shots at some rashly-exposed troops, we descended finally, and were soon afterwards driving towards Courcelles, the nearest German railway station to Metz now available, and from which the line was open to Saarbrück.

Our rough quarters and scanty food at Corny, and the uncertainty of whether for days anything .stirring would occur to break the monotony of the blockade (there was never any bombardment of the works, which the Germans wished to keep intact for themselves) made us decide to stay no longer.

CHAPTER 7

Metz to Brussels, Via Saarbrück

Our drive, from Corny to Courcelles took us over some frightfully rough country roads, and through the villages of Fay, Cuvry, and Fleury (the latter village less than three miles from the scene of the previous day's bloody affair at Peltre), and so across the high road connecting Metz and Strasbourg to Courcelles. The whole of the villages along our route were occupied by German soldiers, who seemed to swarm like locusts over the entire country. As you passed by the bivouac of a regiment of infantry, you came to the picketed horses of cavalry, and then to the parked guns of the artillery, and so on throughout the whole dusty drive.

The eye became wearied of gazing upon these symbols of war, and longed to have something new upon which to rest.

No white tents added beauty to this large encampment of men; and one thing is worthy of remark, that not one single tent, except a large open one erected over some stores, did we see on the trip we have been writing about. Rough huts hastily constructed from boughs of trees, formed stables for the horses, and sometimes shelter for the men, but the latter, when not in the villages, always bivouacked in the open, with no canvas to cover them, and had to construct natural shelter as best they could.

Our papers were examined at every village along the road, but we were detained nowhere, and arrived with a jaded and half-famished horse at Courcelles, a straggling uninviting-looking village, about 5 p. m. At no point had we been able to get a feed for our overworked beast, though the "*Markettenderins*" (*Cantinierès*) of the troops had supplied us once or twice with bread and country wine for ourselves; and now at Courcelles it was evident that not a grain of corn was to be had at the small inns. Courcelles had been converted, by building sheds, &c., into a large provision depot for the army, and it made it all the more tantalizing to see in the open railway station sacks upon sacks of oats piled up, and which one could not touch.

After half-an-hour's exploration, we found also that no lodgings or any sort of cover, except the open railway shed, was to be had; and our faces became blank when we were told by the ticket issuer, who being overworked was not over civil, that no train would go before 8.15 upon the following morning.

But often, when things appear at the worst, the time of improvement begins, and it was so in our case. A good-natured station master, upon hearing our wants, allowed our driver to collect a large sackful of oats from the scattered grains strewn about the yard; and we were also delighted by the news that a train was unexpectedly to go off in a few moments, in which we might find a place.

After seeing our driver walk off with his sack, we contrived to stow ourselves, with half-a-dozen others, in one of the trucks of this train, and were soon on our way to Saarbrück, where we arrived, *via* Forbach, before midnight.

Saarbrück appeared to be an early closing town; not a single hotel was open at that hour; and we were meditating a return to the railway station (after vain attempts to obtain entrance in many quarters), when a man whom we spoke to in a small restaurant, offered us a lodging at his father's house. To go with a perfect stranger to a dirty little house in a side street of a large town, to pass the night there, is not what one finds an agreeable, or would deem, generally, a wise thing; and as our host, after piloting us to our abode, knocked at its door, and it was opened, after two or three enquires of "Who's there?" by a slatternly-looking old woman, we had some misgivings as to whether the railway station would not have been our best decision; but we had by accident lit upon a good Samaritan; slept very peacefully upon two couches until the morning, and then shouldering our knapsacks, set off in search of a guide who would take us to see the scene of the assault of the famous heights of Spicheren.

This we soon found in the person of a private of the *Landwehr*, who had been in Saarbrück at the time of the battle, and to judge from the medals upon his breast had seen several former campaigns. He told us, though, with a sort of candour and want of tendency to brag which one does not often enough meet with, that these had been gained by very slight services, and that he had never been in any general action.

Under his pilotage we crossed the stone bridge over the Saar, a sluggish and deep river, about 50 yards wide, and out along the road, over which the Germans drove the French from the town on the 6th of August. As one crosses the bridge, the heights upon which the Prince Imperial received his "baptism of fire" are in full view; and beyond it, after the town has been cleared, rise on each side the terraced grassy heights, dotted with houses, across which the French skirmishers retired fighting out of the place.

Soon after this, one passes up the hill at the top of which was the first French position at Saarbrück, which was held by them shortly before this battle, but at which no fighting of consequence occurred. This hill is smooth, perhaps 100 feet in height, and of a slope of nearly 15 degrees. Along its crest was a breastwork over which the guns had fired. The earth had been taken from a ditch, about four feet wide, cut in front, and shelter pits for the gunners were made behind.

Between this trench and the main position of the Spicheren heights, stretches for a mile or so along undulating grassy plain, across which runs the French and German boundary line, and which is entirely commanded by the heights beyond. Across this plain the German soldiers had to advance, continually under fire, and gaining no shelter except from the slightly undulating nature of the ground until they arrived pretty close under the Spicheren height itself. For the last half-mile of the advance, our guide told us, the loss was comparatively small, as the French guns had to be depressed a great deal, and the shells, probably fired with too much haste, went over the heads of the assailants.

The hill or heights of Spicheren will always be pointed to as one of the most formidable positions ever attacked and carried in front, since the days of artillery and fire arms.

It is very steep, about 25 degrees, perhaps, in slope, and 150 feet, as far as we could judge, above the plain.

To climb up its side, which is smooth and grassy, except in a few places, was an exertion, and so to carry it in face of a rifle fire from a trench along its summit, and after a long advance exposed to artillery, can be understood to have been a very exceptional feat of arms.

It does not detract from the German bravery to say that the French may be said to have retired before the forces which were turning the height on the right at the same time, and not before those advancing to their front.

The wood on the *French* right of the position was traversed by the

German troops, and the appearance of the latter through it, and on their right flank, naturally made the French unsteady.

If a failure had occurred in the attack made directly over a wide plain, and under such a fire, and against such a position as this, the order for it would have been termed madness, but yet the determined character of the advance had its effect in drawing off the attention of the French from the thick wood on their right, not sufficiently watched, and the fire from which upon their right flank caused their defeat.

From the top of the heights of Spicheren a very fine view can be seen towards Saarbrück, while in the opposite direction (to the south of Forbach) lies a stretch of level plain, over which, after the heights were carried, and the left as well as the right turned, the French retreated in headlong route.

Many crosses to the memory of officers who fell were to be seen on the hill slope, and in the valley, mounds of earth, with an occasional Prussian helmet placed upon a stick thrust into them, marked the resting places of soldiers, but already (not two months after the battle) all traces of the fight, in the way of pieces of shells, accoutrements, &c., had been collected, and little boys moved about selling the *chassepot* and the needle bullets, and offering one relics at about as high a rate of profit, as those at Waterloo offer you the perhaps less genuine souvenirs of the fight that took place there more than half-a-century ago.

After an hour or two spent on the heights we returned to Saarbrück, and at the Hotel Brenner enjoyed the luxury of a good dinner, which one appreciates very decidedly after a day or two's rough fare.

In the evening we walked to the railway station (one of the few buildings, by the way, which bears the marks of the French very nominal bombardment), and left for Treves, where we slept; the next day reaching Brussels by way of Luxembourg, and shortly afterwards crossing the Channel to England.

In the train on our journey to Luxembourg, two English officers, whom we knew, entered our carriage, and with them a French lady, a Countess C——, who had a few days before been to Metz, with the hope of inducing Prince Frederick Charles to let her into the city, with a flag of truce, upon a visit of some special importance to her brother.

She was very kindly treated, she said, and at first permission was granted to her to go in blindfolded, but it was in the end withheld, on the ground of its being a precedent it would not do to create, and so she was travelling back disappointed besides the brother in Metz, she had a father shut up in Paris, and had lost three or four relations in the war. At a railway station some friend spoke to her, and we shall never forget the joy with which she turned to us, and told us of the successful sortie of the 27th (which we have before described), and which her narrator had magnified into a glorious victory for the army of Bazaine. "Now we shall win; we *must* win!" she exclaimed; and none of us had the heart to undeceive her, and dim her happiness before its time.

Our travels among the scenes of the war were; now over, and so our stories about them cease. That these may have interested our readers as much as what we saw and experienced did us, we can hardly venture to hope.

www.ingramcontent.com/pod-product-compliance
Lightning Source LLC
Chambersburg PA
CBHW021101090426
42738CB00006B/444